· · ·

On Drama

THEATER: Theory/Text/Performance

Enoch Brater, Series Editor

Recent Titles:

On Drama

Boundaries of Genre, Borders of Self

Michael Goldman

Ann Arbor

The University of Michigan Press

2003   2002   2001   2000   4   3   2   1

*A CIP catalog record for this book is available
from the British Library.*

Library of Congress Cataloging-in-Publication Data

Goldman, Michael, 1936–
    On drama : boundaries of genre, borders of self /
Michael Goldman.
        p.   cm. — (Theater—theory/text/performance)
    Includes bibliographical references and index.
    ISBN 0-472-11011-X (acid-free paper)
    1. Drama—History and criticism. 2. Literary form.
I. Title. II. Series.
PN1631 .G59   2000
808.2—dc21   00-008697

• • •

for Eleanor

• • •

Est-ce toi, Nomade,
qui nous passeras ce soir aux rives du réel?

—ST.-JOHN PERSE

Enter a gentle Astringer.

—SHAKESPEARE

Acknowledgments

I would never have thought of writing about the subject of genre if it hadn't been for Elise Garrison, who graciously asked me to speak to the conference on genre she organized at Texas A & M in 1994. And I might never have had the courage to write this book if not for LeAnn Fields at the University of Michigan Press and for Enoch Brater who, among other, more celebrated services to dramatic scholarship, directs the Press's Theater: Theory/Text/Performance series. Michigan was the natural place to look when I realized the plan in my head was for something this (let us call it) unconventional in length, shape, and content. Without their encouragement, I don't think I would have undertaken it.

I'm also deeply grateful to the friends and colleagues who have read and commented on the manuscript at various stages: Michael Cadden, Joyce Carol Oates, Joanna Picciotto, Jennie Snyder. For particular advice at crucial points, my thanks go to Stephen Daitz, Jim Moyer, and Nancy Selleck.

I also want to thank the students in two graduate courses, English 560 at Princeton and English G6725x at Columbia, where a number of the ideas in this book were first tested and certainly refined in what were for me exciting and memorable sessions.

Acknowledgments

Finally, my greatest and happiest debt, as ever, is to my wife, Eleanor Bergstein, true friend, great love, and absolute editor, for this and everything, sharper phrases, deeper thoughts, an inexpressibly better and happier life.

• • •

I want to propose a way of thinking about drama—its power, its solace, its strangeness—that begins as a way of thinking about genre. In the end I hope to be able to say something new about the role drama plays in our lives, its status as a unique imaginative instrument, its power to address certain trepidations that have darkened contemporary thought. But I need to begin with genre. And I must first confront the fact that for many drama lovers the topic of genre, even the word *genre* itself, is likely to produce a chilling effect, a kind of eye-rolling impatience or dissatisfaction, which I have to admit I share. Clearly, I confess this with some eagerness—because I think the very distaste that the topic can inspire gives us an unexpected clue to the role played by genre in the experience of drama.

Let me focus briefly on some possible reasons for this distaste. First, there is something inescapably pedantic about the topic. It's hard not to feel that Shakespeare's attitude toward genre is expressed in his portrait of Polonius. "Tragedy, comedy, history, pastoral, pastoral-comical, historical-pastoral, tragical-historical, tragical-comical-historical-pastoral!" The sense that genre carries with it of exclusion, of the policing of boundaries may seem out of place in the neighborhood of art.

At the same time, there's something incoherent about the term. English departments, like my own, often offer introductory courses that promise to treat "each of the genres"—and by that they mean poetry, fiction, and drama. (Autobiography, criticism, "non-fiction," don't seem in this context quite to be genres, though they may *have* them.) Specialists in drama, of course, are usually more concerned with distinguishing genres within drama, particularly comedy and tragedy. But *are* they within drama? Can we comfortably say that comedy and tragedy are subgenres of drama? And what of those very different types to which the term *subgenre* is normally applied? Are they in fact subordinate, contained in some sense within the larger generic types? Is revenge tragedy a subgenre of tragedy as, say, the Petrarchan sonnet is a subform of the sonnet? Possibly, but what, then, of the detective thriller? *The Mousetrap* may be a kind of comedy, but is it a subgenre of comedy or a mixed genre, like tragicomedy, say? And what does it mean to talk of mixed or alternative genres?

Part of the problem is a curious lack of symmetry and coordination of scale between generic designations. If comedy and tragedy divide the world, or even some part of a world, how do they divide it—80–20? 70–30? If I adapt an Agatha Christie novel for the stage, at what level am I changing genre? Tragical-comical-historical-pastoral: is that one, presumably mixed genre, one mixed genre combined with one subgenre, a series of genres rapidly replacing each other, or what? At this point one's tempted to exclaim with Berowne

Those earthly godfathers of heaven's lights
That give a name to every fixed star
Get no more profit of their shining nights
Than those that walk and wot not what they are.

Now, one might well reply to Berowne that if you know the stars' names you are likely to notice and remember their positions better and that distinguishing between stars and planets may be useful as well as pleasing. And one might at this point simply conclude that it would be better to be guided through the night skies of genre by someone less buffaloed by generic astronomy than I appear to be. There are of course other, more technical ways of dealing with the subject than I have so far advanced, ways less disturbed by the confusions of everyday language. And I'm well aware of the value of such discussions, historical and theoretical, which this study of course is not intended to replace.

Still, most of these discussions, certainly the most influential, are deficient in a signal respect. They fail to engage drama fully as an experience, an ongoing moment-to-moment process for audiences or readers. They have in common a tendency to treat genre as a reflective category, a way of classifying and systematizing dramatic texts and performances after the fact. Everything changes, however, if we stop to think of genre as not entirely unlike rhyme, say, or ambiguity, as a feature, that is, whose primary interest for readers or audiences is as something that *happens* to us in a poem or play, *as* it happens.

True, this aspect of genre seldom goes entirely unmentioned in treatments of the subject, but it is usually so subordinate as to be effectively suppressed. Let me illustrate with what are arguably two of the most incisive contemporary discussions. Each offers a valuable insight but ignores the direct moment-to-moment apprehension of genre as part of the experience of a work of art. Derrida recognizes that there is a radical instability in the idea of genre but sees it as a feature inherent to any taxonomic system. It is a salutary point, though its bent, as Derrida handles it, is to make the concept of genre vanish, like all concepts, down a deconstructive wormhole. The great problem with Derrida's analysis is that it obscures much that is important about the way genre functions in our experience of the arts, especially of drama. For our purposes it's more valuable to see that, as it operates in drama, the instability of genre has a specific and unique texture. We experience it not only as something that happens to us when we try to arrange dramas according to a coherent system of classification but, rather, as part of our ongoing recognition of what's happening in the theater.

Similarly, Alastair Fowler's very useful and certainly correct point that genre is *not* taxonomic, that genres are not classes, is equally after the fact, because in the heat of the moment we respond to genre *as if* it were taxonomical, as if it were an expression of a coordinated system of types and subtypes—as if it helped us to recognize and place something within a border, within a map of borders. Fowler says that genre is not a class but a type and as such is not concerned with boundaries. He's right, if one thinks of genre as something supplied after the fact—"What was that?" But as an effect—"What *is* that?"—when we become aware of it as a phenomenon of performance or reading, genre does not obey so simple a logic. We experience it as something looming or fading, definite or disrupted, something more like expectation or occasion—a weather, an attitude, a mood. Yet, as such, it involves a sensation like that of classification, of boundaries anticipated and apprehended.

So there may be some value in turning to a more rough and ready testimony. Indeed, I'd like to suggest that both my own uneasiness with the idea of genre and the troublesome role that the term seems to play in more-or-less ordinary conversation can be put to use, can in fact be revealing about the nature of drama and help put us freshly in touch with the design and imaginative life of many plays, especially those that seem to foreground or problematize generic questions.

What I'm stalking under the cover of genre is the human weight of the processes of drama—what drama as a special kind of social practice does for and with our lives. These reflections will keep turning toward and away from the idea of genre, a winding, sometimes hairpin route that I hope will come to seem appropriate to the oblique and unstable way in which genre itself operates in drama. I offer them as a kind of prologue to what may be possible in thinking about drama, especially at this cultural moment.

It seems to me that we are at a juncture when a special kind of urgency, even of primacy, may be claimed for the study of drama—for the process of thinking about the power and complexity and cultural importance of great plays. This book addresses that urgency and attempts to justify it. I hope, in what follows, that, by moving between some salient features of the genre we call drama and the problems I find in thinking about both genre in general and the genres we normally *associate* with drama, our understanding of drama itself and of the operation of a range of remarkable plays may be enhanced. Through this I hope to make a contribution to the theory of drama and to critical method but above all to address some of the unique ways in which drama speaks to and enlarges our experience.

For the purposes of this study I'm going to be considering the idea of genre only as it applies to drama. But, though it's convenient to put the apparently more general issue of literary genre to one side, it would be a grave mistake to assume that the issue of literary genre *is* the general issue—to assume, that is, that literature is the larger category, of which drama is a specialization. Many problems not only in dramatic but literary theory would take on a sharply new perspective if, just to clear the air, let us say, we were to reverse the process and think instead of drama as the most general case of literature, with poetry, the novel, and so forth as specializations. We might do well in fact to imagine drama as the originary literary or artistic form, if only to offset the myth, nowadays unacknowledged because epistemologically incorrect, but nevertheless still dominant, of the literary origins of drama (from choral lyric, narrative, Solonic speeches in the agora, or whatever). Actually, the old habit of thinking about drama as a genre of "literature," a habit seemingly as old as criticism itself, has worked to obscure some important connections between drama and life—especially with some features of life we're likely today to regard as intensely difficult, issues that bear on self and meaning, on persons and texts, on identity and community. Some consequences of such a change of perspective will be suggested in what follows.

Clearly, the first function of genre is that it be recognized. This immediately involves genre with one of the most peculiar of dramatic-theoretical categories: recognition. What *always* gets recognized in a play? One thing must be its genre. Whatever genre may be, its function is to be recognized. If it's tragedy or comedy or mixed, we recognize it; if we can't recognize the genre, we recognize *that*. And, of course, above everything we recognize that what we are attending to is drama, not a novel or poem. But this means that there's another thing we always recognize in a play—the presence of acting. Even if we are only reading a play, our sense of it as drama depends on our knowledge that there is such a thing as theatrical performance. And in the theater, to recognize that what we are watching is drama, we must recognize acting when we see it. It's not that we say, oh, there's Ian McKellen or Anna Deveare Smith—but we do say that's good or bad acting, or at least we say that acting is going on; inside the role we recognize an actor.

Recognition is a peculiar category, and one of the most peculiar questions that it raises is whether it is peculiarly dramatic. It crops up at the very beginning of dramatic theory and in a nonobvious way. Aristotle rides the term; he seizes on it far more than appears to be necessary, and as a result *recognition* historically has continued to get attached to drama, and to literature in general, in senses very different from what Aristotle meant.

It's tempting to explain Aristotle's emphasis on recognition by an intuition on his part of those broader, more modern meanings of the term—awareness, understanding, discovery, insight, etc. And I think there is in fact some such intuition about drama operating in the *Poetics,* and not merely Aristotle's awareness of how frequently discoveries about *philia,* family bonds, occur in Athenian tragedy. We shall see how recognitions of the broader sort are connected to the unique human urgencies of drama. I'm inclined, however, to attach Aristotle's insistence on recognition to another, even more peculiar emphasis that occurs at the very beginning of the *Poetics* and which is apparently dropped, or at least not followed up, in the rest of the treatise, the connection between imitation and knowledge.

Early in the *Poetics* Aristotle addresses the question of why people seem to take pleasure in imitation per se, even if the object imitated is unpleasant. His answer is that we love knowledge, that people love to learn. Admittedly, the question about imitation is basic to any study of tragedy. Admittedly, too, we may feel that Aristotle's answer is rather too much the kind that a teacher would be inclined to give, and Aristotle indeed seems to make little of it in the discussion that follows. But there is, in this first mention of imitation, an implicit connection to the importance of recognition: at the climactic point of a tragedy, there's discovery, and, even if it's a discovery of terrible or ugly things, it's part of the satisfying tragic climax.

Recognition is a topic that well illustrates the dangers of thinking about drama as a subcategory of literature, as a genre *of* literature. Recognition has a unique inflection in the theater because it is connected with a psychological mechanism that also achieves a unique theatrical prominence, the mechanism we call *identification.* Ultimately, the question of how recognition relates to genre is of interest because it leads us to this mechanism, which is at the heart of drama's generic appeal.

We may make headway here in the study of genre by thinking about the *Bacchae,* a play that offers a particularly brilliant investigation of the complex dynamics of recognition and identification in the theater. With the possible exception of *Hamlet,* no play more boldly identifies itself *with* drama and with the most famous genre of drama than the *Bacchae,* where the god of the theater himself sets the tragedy in motion.

Think of an actor stepping forward to present himself as Dionysus at the beginning of this play. Remember that the Greek actor is a high civic official, a priest of the god officiating at a public event, and also a contestant for a major prize:

> I am Dionysus, the son of Zeus,
> come back to Thebes, the land where I was born.
> My mother was Cadmus' daughter, Semele by
>   name,
> midwived by fire, delivered by the lightning's
> blast.

　　　And here I stand, a god incognito,
disguised as man, beside the stream of Dirce
and the waters of Ismenus. There before the palace
I see my lightning-married mother's grave,
and there upon the ruins of her shattered house
the living fire of Zeus still smolders on
in deathless witness of Hera's violence and rage
against my mother.

Dionysus' prologue offers multiple "identifications" in both of two large senses ordinarily given to the word: (1) presentation of one's identity (as in "Identify yourself!"; and (2) taking on or sympathizing with the traits or feelings of another person. Here is a man, an actor, playing a god who has disguised himself as a man so that he may be revealed as a god. Dionysus tells us that he wants to be recognized by the city as a god, but he wants to be recognized on behalf of his human mother, and he plans to achieve this by destroying his mother's enemies, just as his father god destroyed his mother by appearing in his undisguised identity to answer her desire.

　　Dionysus reaches us at this moment as a braid of competing yet coherent self-projections. He identifies-with both his father, Zeus, and his mother, Semele. He passionately enters into her sufferings and the insults to her honor, but he makes clear he wishes to be Zeus-like, and to be seen as Zeus-like, in punishment. He defines himself in terms of opposition as well as allegiance to both gods and men. He is at once an exotic stranger from the east and a son of Thebes returning home. He is both god and man, insider and outsider, torn and whole, masculine and feminine, barbarian and Greek, the product, according to legend, of both a mother's and a father's womb.

The inflected Greek of the opening lines emphasizes these multiple vectors, the different directions that the speaking "I" is coming from. Simply to say "I . . . Dionysus" is to bracket a range of identifications:

Heko Dios pais tinde Tebaion Kthona
Dionysos

[I-am (here), Zeus' child, (back) in this Theban land Dionysus]

The complex and multiple identifications at play in this speech were well caught in the Performance Group's celebrated version of the play *Dionysus in '69*. Every night the actor who was to play Dionysus greeted the audience:

> Good evening. I see you found your seats. My name is Joan MacIntosh, daughter of Walter Macintosh and June Wyatt. I was born twenty-three years ago in a hospital in Newark, New Jersey. I have come here tonight for three very important reasons. The first and most important is to announce my divinity. I am a god. The second of these reasons is to establish my rites and rituals. As you can see, they are already in progress. And the third is to be born, if you'll excuse me.

As befits the god of the theater, all Dionysus' identifications exaggerate the basic doubleness of the actor.

This doubleness springs, of course, from the actor's status as someone who is most forcibly defined by taking on the definition of someone else. Frequently in the *Bacchae,* we feel the presence of Dionysus when other characters take on some aspect of his identity, which then shifts and alters definition within them. This is especially true of the Chorus, whose energies often spring in Greek drama from impersonations that riffle across the surface of the text and lend themselves to the broad racing embodiments of dance. At various times the Bacchae act out not only the Zeus and Semele phases of Dionysus' story but the roles of rabid beasts, suckling cubs, fleeing gazelles, and also the hounds that hunt them. Once, after they have grown upset and been calmed by Dionysus, Euripides introduces a Messenger, who then vividly describes a mirroring group of calm Theban Bacchantes. After having evoked them, however, as sober, peaceful, exhausted, at rest, the Messenger goes on to more agitated personations. He first describes a group of Theban shepherds who, stirred up by an outsider, attack the women, "hunting" them, and then describes the rage of the women, who turn (like "hounds") on their pursuers, running amok, setting them to flight, and finally tearing apart animals and even children with their bare hands. Oscillating in his identifications between hunter and hunted, animal and human, the Messenger thus proleptically enacts for us the play's whole horrible story of male and female madness, his speech a run-up to Agave's climactic appearance with the severed head of Pentheus, the son she has murdered. Dionysus' braid of identifications ravels and unravels across the performance of the entire play.

Why should audiences enjoy this kind of thing? It's suggestive that, when Pentheus worries about being seen in women's dress in Thebes, Dionysus assures him that the streets he passes through will be empty. The usual city crowds have vanished, and the implication is that in the same way the city of Athens has emptied out today to crowd into the theater of Dionysus to watch and share these rhythmed, contagious, competing identifications. What, then, is Euripides suggesting about drama's appeal? Have we come to the theater in search of an elevating civic exercise, or have we left our normal haunts to go crazy over Dionysus?

Dionysus' project of revealing himself is typical of drama in general. Consider how important to any dramatic process is the showing forth of the performer hidden in the role. Whatever rhetoric of self-erasure, of "losing oneself in the part," may prevail at any historical moment, audiences go to the theater expecting and wanting to watch actors acting. Even if this seems to require (as in Method acting) that they "disappear" into their roles, the actors in fact never quite disappear. (If they did, as Stanley Cavell points out, we would not be watching a play but having an hallucination.) In the theater we respond to the rhythm, grace, power, charm, mimetic skill, of the actors, to the music of their performance. We tend to echo the actors' persuasive imita-

tions in our own bodies—even as Dionysus first makes
his identity known, as he tells us, by communicating his
"dances to the feet of living men."

The showing forth promised by the actors extends
also to the larger processes of the play, such as plot or
action. For these too are brought to life by acting. We
usually come to the theater not only to see actors performing, but to see something happening to and through
the characters that the actors present. This something
we often call *action,* and it involves what we could easily
call *revelation*—pretty much in the same sense that the
Poetics seems to impart to the catchy word *recognition.*
We also usually come to watch the showing forth of
some agent across the action. That is, we expect to see at
least one actor press forward the identity of her character toward some kind of defining climax or memorable
cumulative self-presentation, to which we expect to
respond with some quickening of heart or mind.

And indeed Dionysus makes this his goal. He
promises us in the prologue that before the play is over
he will stand revealed, his identity made manifest to
every man in the city. But the *Bacchae* is nowhere more
theoretical, nowhere more self-consciously engaged
with the nature of drama—and nowhere more ironic—
than in its treatment of this revelation. For Dionysus to
make himself known in a way that he finds satisfying, by
means of an action that wins him the kind of recognition
he feels he deserves, his play will have to disturb some
deeply held notions about tragic recognition. In doing
so, it taps into some of the most painful ironies of family

and social life. These ironies have to do with recognition and identification but also with our perception of genre.

The revelation Dionysus seeks, the climactic moment of recognition, will only be possible after he has wildly agitated his onstage audience, has visited madness upon his followers. It's a commonplace that this climax is an archetype of the tragic pattern, with its *sparagmos* of Pentheus, the horrified recognition of Agave, and the showing-forth of Dionysus. But it's a climax which strangely calls the point of the whole tragic process into question, especially the role played in it by recognition.

The *Bacchae* is at first glance generically uncompli-cated—tragedy in 200-proof form—but it complicates its impact by undermining what might be called the generic pretensions of tragedy at the very instant—again a paradigmatic instant—of "tragic recognition." The cli-mactic moment of recognition in the *Bacchae* comes when Agave realizes that in a frenzy of religious ecstasy she has killed her son. The scene is unmistakably meta-dramatic, a curious and horrible mingling of the roles of performer and audience, as a mother who was a per-former of Dionysus' rite becomes audience to the fate of her son, who was lured into fatal performance and female disguise because he longed to watch.

Though the *Bacchae* precedes Aristotle, one wonders if some version of the catharsis theory, perhaps one that stressed even more than Aristotle does the achievement of healthy mental balance, wasn't already something of a commonplace by the time the play was written, because Euripides seems to be parodying the idea of catharsis at the very moment of Agave's discovery. This is a moment when, to its age, the play might seem to be coalescing into a textbook example of its genre—tragedy doing its famous cathartic thing just where it was supposed to, presided over by Dionysus himself. Cadmus puts Agave through a veritable checklist of the mind-cleansing symptoms of catharsis:

> CADMUS: First raise your eyes to the heavens.
> AGAVE: There.
>   But why?
> CADMUS: Does it look the same as it did before?
>   Or has it changed?
> AGAVE: It seems—somehow—clearer,
>   brighter than it was before.
> CADMUS: Do you still feel
>   the same flurry inside you?
> AGAVE: The same—flurry?
>   No, I feel—somehow —calmer. I feel as
>   though—
>   my mind were somehow—changing . . .
> CADMUS: Whose head do you hold in your hands?

Calm of mind, all passion spent. But the result is only to let her see unbearable, irremediable horror with perfect clarity—a horror that Dionysus will quickly extend to Thebes for generations to come. Recognition, and by extension tragedy itself, isn't necessarily good for you, whatever the theorists say. Writing at the end of the Peloponnesian War, Euripides may have been challenging the entire pious civic justification of the Dionysian festival.

· II ·

Years ago I suggested that identification could be considered the covert theme of drama. I was offering by that to redefine the casual use of the term we employ when we speak of actors "identifying" with a character or audiences identifying with actors. I suggested that we should instead think of identification as processual, the making or doing of identity. The actor *acts* an identity, puts it together before our eyes, sustains it, thrusts it forward toward our attention, keeps it coherent (not necessarily consistent) in the face of obstacles and difficulties. So in the theater we are always keenly aware of a practice of identity shaping and projection. We enter into it and are engaged by it, we feel it as plastic, sensuous, exciting, something achieved across the demands and resistances of script and performance. It should not be surprising, then, that the process of identification in this sense—of establishing a self that in some way transcends the normal confusions of self—is remarkably current as a theme in plays of all types from all periods, from *Oedipus* to *Earnest* to *Cloud Nine*. "The action of any play, all that its characters 'go through,' is a way of discharging and expressing the hidden burden of threat that these confusions always carry."

I still think that this is a basic way in which the action of plays tends to reproduce the acting process. But I now think this theory needs to be developed by taking into

account the way "identification" in the precise psychoanalytical sense inevitably involves confusion about identity. As Diana Fuss points out in *Identification Papers,* the
psychoanalytical process of identification, by its very
nature, must act to *destabilize* identity, to render identity
contradictory or incomplete. Identification involves
crossing the boundaries between self and other, outside
and inside. I identify with my father, my mother, my
friend; I identify with others or images of others, with
moments and modes and gestures of self-presentation I
see in the world outside me. We identify by introjec-
tion, by incorporating the other in whole or in part. To
go back to the two ordinary-language meanings of
identification I mentioned earlier: identifying oneself,
establishing an independent identity, depends on identi-
fying-with others. But there's an inevitable tension
between the two, a continual setting up and violation of
barriers.

The self, in this account, is an inherently self-under-
mining amalgam. The sentiment of continuity and
responsibility we attach to the word *I,* the center, however we name it, of memory and agency from which we
seem to operate, is composed of entities that threaten its
safety and satisfaction, not to mention coherence. Our
identity is constructed out of beings whom we desire,
fear, surrender to, recoil from, pursue—beings faster or
slower than our heartbeat. The thing we most like to
think of as snugly and stably inside us is made up of those
things that are hottest and coldest around our borders.
How hard it is to separate Dionysus from his god-intox-

icated mother or Pentheus from his. Dionysus and Pentheus not only double each other in their feminized garments and behavior; they both mirror with bewildering interchangeability the identifications made by Semele and Agave, who themselves take on—and are destroyed by—the powers and pleasures of an absent/present Other, a hidden/revealed god. Dionysus' prologue, then, with its many roles and self-descriptions, is not only a model of theatrical performance but of the tense, unstable transactions of identification itself.

Indeed, nothing is more revealing about the cultural force of drama than the way identification and imitation are linked to recognition in the earliest stages of infant development. Both identity and imitation seem to be born out of the "mutual gaze" described by developmental psychologists. The emotional life of the infant depends on this linked and braided exchange of looks with his mother. Perhaps most important for our purposes, clinical study of the mutual gaze reveals that it involves not a single stable mood or aspect but a series of rapidly altering perspectives.

Theatrical performance insists on a crucial aspect of identification that is perfectly clear from this kind of infant observation but often lost sight of by official psychology—the fact that identification is an ongoing action. One of our most dangerous mental habits is to think of identification in the past tense. Though it may be true that identifications, like everything else, originate in the past, the burden of identification as a process falls in the present quite as much, say, as the burden of acting or

speaking. While it is useful to remind us, as psychoanalysis does, of the disturbing alterity of our own identities by locating our identifications in external, remote
sources, in other persons and spaces and particularly
other times—in childhood excitements, "ghosts of the
past," the parents and portents of our infancy—this kind
of discussion may blind us to the truth that our
significant identifications are all here, within us, and acting now.

Theater actively feeds on this most private and hidden
of daily processes. In ordinary life the ongoing process of
identification is so volatile, complex, and improvised
that we habitually conceal it. We become adept at projecting an icon of ourselves, a readable mask that covers
the moment-by-moment turbulence of our identifications. How different this is from the way an actor
dons, wields, comments on, animates, modifies, the
changing masks of performance. The way I, as an actor,
identify my character to a theater audience is, in fact,
more like the complex way I identify myself to myself
than the relatively guarded way I identify myself to others. Though any actor's performance must also be readable, masklike, to some degree, still the exigencies of
action, character, and the projective physics of presentation combine to heighten our awareness of the tremen-
dous, multiple energies of identification at play in any
theatrical moment.

Furthermore, if there is, in the action of any good
play, some tension or difficulty in the actorlike establish-
ment of identity that the chief characters undertake,

there is also, in any good actor's performance, a definiteness of projected identity, a presentation of self that seems surer and sharper than anything we encounter in ordinary life. One of the things that makes theater appealing is the way these projected identities seem contagious, the way they prompt us to identifications. Subliminally, we pick up and echo the actor's process; we may find ourselves comfortably walking and talking like one of the characters when we leave.

Now, it's well-known that the actor's singular freedom to shift identities not only makes him a cynosure but inspires fear and apprehension, what Jonas Barish calls the antitheatrical prejudice. The ratio of attraction to aversion varies from society to society, but some mixture of the two is a basic motor of drama. My account of identification suggests, however, that the attraction is connected to the aversion in a complicated way, not only through the relatively simple mechanism of suppressed desire but also at a deeper level of identity formation. The pull that the audience, Pentheus-like, feels toward incorporating the actor's identifications stimulates anxiety, not only because certain identifications are "forbidden" but because the very pleasure of watching a performance heightens the threatening movement across internal boundaries that all identification involves. Its power is compelling because identification is the fluid source of the very self-definition it now threatens to disarrange. It reactivates a buried volatility that we normally keep tightly controlled. Not I-am-becoming-somebody-else but I-am-becoming-somebody-else-*yet again.*

It is Nietzsche, in a little noticed passage, who catches the unique connection between identification and the uncanny power of drama when he describes the typical recognition scene as a return from the dead. Nietzsche suggests that such scenes provide a boost, a kind of feedback circuit for the basic energy that flows through any effective dramatic performance. In his view any dramatic recognition echoes and reinforces the surprising, energizing and at base deeply unsettling engagement we feel in the presence of acting. The reason is that in the theater we respond to a connection between what the actor is doing and our own processes of identification.

For Nietzsche theater originates at the moment when Dionysus becomes enacted rather than imagined, but to describe the crucial importance of that transformation he turns not to the *Bacchae* or Dionysus but to Euripides' *Alcestis,* to King Admetus, who sees his wife returning from the dead. This thrilling, terrifying moment is comparable, Nietzsche says, to what happened whenever the Athenian spectator saw the tragic actor:

> Consider Admetus as he is brooding over the memory of his recently departed wife Alcestis, consuming himself in her spiritual contemplation, when suddenly a similarly formed, similarly walking woman's figure is led toward him, heavily veiled; let us imagine his sudden trembling unrest, his tempestuous comparisons, his instinctive conviction—and

we have an analogy with what the spectator felt in his Dionysian excitement when he saw the approach on the stage of the god with whose sufferings he had already identified himself. Involuntarily, he transferred the whole magic image of the god that was trembling before his soul to that masked figure and, as it were, dissolved its reality into the unreality of spirits.

This is a complex, powerful, and precise theoretical formula. Watching an actor is like seeing the inside of your head walking toward you. Admetus is overwhelmed by the approach of someone who appears to be his dead wife, Alcestis—because she already plays a consuming role in his imagination. The actor projects into physical reality a figure already active in our intimate mental life; to see the actor-as-character is like discovering that someone close to you has returned from the dead. The actor assumes an identity that has the uncanny force of one of our identifications. She becomes, like Dionysus, a *revenant* brought home to us in a walking, talking body.

For Nietzsche this is the basic theatrical phenomenon from the point of view of the audience—to see *oneself* transformed into an actor:

This process of the tragic chorus is the *dramatic* proto-phenomenon: to see oneself transformed before one's own eyes and to begin to act as if one had actually entered into another body, another character. This process stands at the beginning of the origin of drama.

Recognitions can of course play a role in advancing any narrative. But recognitions have a unique status in drama because they echo and amplify the basic excitement of theatrical performance, the fear and attraction associated with acting—with the uncannily embodied play of the competing figures out of which identity is formed.

The potency of dramatic recognitions, then, is that they threaten as well as stabilize, threaten even as they stabilize. Why can such moments move us so? They are not simply resolution points, places where the plot turns or straightens out, but surges of energy. They draw on the subversive dynamics of identification, the psychologically charged presence of the actor. The ghost walks, the tomb opens, things that are supposed to be inside get out, the brother you thought you had accidentally killed comes back, solid and smiling, the arrow still fixed in his eye socket . . . Comedy may at times reverse the affect by suffusing the recognition with an access of fantastic safety ("My long lost brother!" "Gwendolen, at last!"), but the comfort of the safety reflects the power of the fear. Many of the most intricate recognition scenes in comedy reverse fantasies of sexual threat that have been carefully elaborated over the course of the play, as in *Measure for Measure, Cymbeline,* or Marivaux's *The Triumph of Love.* How wonderful to discover as Agis does in *Triumph* that the apparent female enemy, plotting against you, the killer of your father, is in fact none of these but instead the lost mother who loves you and who will give you a kingdom and a bride. The recognitions of *Measure,* with the all-knowing Duke judging, pardoning, and bringing couples together, succeed, as Meredith Skura points out, in restoring the distinction between sexual pleasure and punishment, between marriage and execution, that the play has till now so darkly blurred. The comic energy comes not directly from recognition but from recognition being channeled so as to reward our desires with unlikely and surprising protection. The genius of the *Alcestis* is to give us both the festive comic version of a return from the dead and its uncanny underside. Nietzsche's genius in writing about that play is to see Admetus' moment of recognition as a defining instance of the uncanniness of theater. In comedy quite as much as tragedy, recognition scenes draw their force from the destabilizing energies of acting. As with Oedipus or Agave, to discover the identity of an Other who defines you, an Other who you are, is always a possible prelude to horror. It's the last thing we want, but we want it from theater.

III

This view of recognition suggests something interesting about the function of genres in drama. For, while genre clearly *is* about boundaries, the sensing of boundaries, the policing of boundaries, it seems also to be the case that it's about the permeation of boundaries. Again, this is not a question of the logical or semiological implications of the concept but of what an audience can recognize in the present moment of performance. It would be hard to overestimate the extent to which drama involves the violation or testing of genre boundaries. Genre as a system of expectations or signals seems to facilitate or invite penetration of its own implied defenses. Most if not all good plays to some extent regularly readjust their generic boundaries, as with Shakespeare's scapegoats and the frequently uncooperative manner of their going—the minority reports of a Malvolio, a Shylock, a Don Armado—or characters like Osric in *Hamlet* or the snake-bearing Clown in *Antony* who are in no sense "comic relief" but, rather, messengers from across the boundaries of genre.

(Perhaps the most mysterious of these is the "Gentle Astringer," a character who appears out of nowhere near the end of *All's Well That Ends Well* to help the heroine to the happy ending that this often sour comedy continually solicits and erodes. He gives his assistance and disappears, his very name a puzzle for the ages. Is he "A gentleman, a stranger" or a Gentle Ostringer [a conjecture only marginally more comprehensible than Astringer— the word may mean "goshawk-keeper"]? Easily confused with a misprint, he seems to materialize out of the script itself just long enough to add an unnecessary mediator to the comic process while the stage fills yet again with talk of age and doubt and death.)

In Shakespeare climaxes are often marked by a cross-genre event. In *Love's Labor's Lost* Marcade arrives with news of the French king's death at the moment when the comic game of mistaken identities and sexual combat has reached a peak of animation. The ridiculous pageant of the Nine Worthies, presented by the lovers to distract attention from their own embarrassment, turns into a brawl with the news that Jaquenetta is pregnant:

> *Enter a messenger,* Monsieur Marcade.
> MARCADE: God save you, madam.
> PRINCESS: Welcome, Marcade,
> But that thou interrupt'st our merriment.

Shakespeare, in this early play, goes on to address quite explicitly the question of genre limits and boundaries:

> Worthies, away! The scene begins to cloud.

> To move wild laughter in the throat of death,
> It is impossible.

> Our wooing doth not end like an old play;
> Jack hath not Jill.

That's too long for a play.

Marcade is only the most explicit manifestation of a permeability to the anticomic that runs through Shakespearean comedy. We misunderstand his so-called scapegoat figures if we think that they are expelled so that the comedy can go on. They are there not to protect but to enlarge the comic ambit. The coherence of the comedy depends on the cares and stresses the play measures itself against and manages to include without losing its identity. Our sense of Shakespearean comedy as a bounded, identifiable realm of experience owes much to the evocation of a crossable border by these figures who come and go, as at a long, motley party, with news of an "inappropriate" kind.

Indeed, the pulsing across the apparent boundaries of genre that we recognize in the Marcades and Malvolios is usually also prefigured in Shakespeare at the very beginning of a comedy, when festivities are typically initiated by a rejection or resistance to festivity:

> In sooth I know not why I am so sad.
> (*Merchant of Venice*)

> —I pray thee, Rosalind, Sweet my coz, be merry.
> —Dear Celia, I show more mirth than I am mistress of.
> (*As You Like It*)

As with Olivia's mourning in *Twelfth Night* or the vast program of renunciation announced at the beginning of

Love's Labor's Lost, resistance to comedy functions in Shakespeare as a recognition of comedy's power, an invitation to extend its scope.

Similarly in tragedy it's not the simple contrast provided by the clowns that intensifies the tragic mood but their specific access to that which has apparently been excluded in making the mood available. Rather than a "relief," these playful or foolish visitants widen the mortal seriousness of the play. The gravedigger hands Hamlet a skull, Osric delivers a fatal challenge, the yokel brings Cleopatra the asp, the Porter after a night of heavy drinking announces that Macbeth's castle has been converted into Hell.

Nor is the play of genres limited to contrasts between tragedy and comedy. *Romeo and Juliet,* for example, makes us aware of movement between alternative generic notions of tragedy. Early in the play the most recognizable markers of genre are a series of references to fatality and foreboding that seem almost laboriously introduced:

A pair of star-crossed lovers . . .

The fearful passage of their death-marked love . . .

> My mind misgives
> Some consequence yet hanging in the stars
> Shall bitterly begin his fearful date . . .

Two points should be remembered about this heavy underlining. First, the references to fate, though they

originate with the Chorus, soon come to rest with
Romeo. Second, Romeo's fatalistic view turns out not
to be his play's. As the drama unfolds, the tragedy-as-
fatality markers are swallowed up by, and ultimately
function by making more intense, the play's accelerating
sense of tragedy-as-contingency.

Not surprisingly, Shakespeare helps us to see the
functional permeability of genre with unusual clarity.
But the supple, reversible generic topology I have been
describing contributes to the dramatic weight of all kinds
of plays by all sorts of authors. Everywhere we look we
find this process, by which one generic understanding
both penetrates and contains another, usually by means
of the very gesture that apparently insists on their separation.

For example, no sooner has *Tamburlaine* begun with a
firm statement of what its "tragic glass" will exclude—

> From jigging veins of rhyming mother wits
> And such conceits as clownage keeps in pay
> We'll lead you to the stately tent of war

—than it takes us *to* a mother wit, Mycetes, who speaks
in a jigging vein. Again, this may seem to be a mere contrast; the play regularly defines its hero by what he is
not. But the series of ineffectual rulers, the cowardly
son, the melting virgins, also work much more directly
to project Tamburlaine's theatrical power. Especially in
Part One they compose a sequence of daring sado-
masochistic appropriations. Like the heaped corpses, the

maidens hung up in chains and shot with arrows, the captive kings harnessed to Tamburlaine's chariot, they all become "sights of power" as he calls them, figures whose mana he magically absorbs.

Of course, every play refigures its apparent generic boundaries in its own way. The First Part of *Tamburlaine* accomplishes a trick seldom repeated in the history of drama (*Le Cid* is the only comparable example I can think of), by which success achieves the force of tragedy. By this I mean that the eventual triumph of the hero gets combined with the energy of facing, amid the pleasures of theater, the worst the mind can contemplate, and thus taking on the mood of severe urgency one associates with tragedy. Then, in Part Two we get the further trick by which even death becomes part of the triumphal procession. Tamburlaine in death manages to remain the great absorber of opposition.

Reinforcing the effect of generic expansion that Marlowe achieves in this play is a negotiation between medieval and modern applications of the word *tragic*. In one sense the tragic glass of *Tamburlaine* simply shows us the fall of kings—the medieval descent from high to low—over and over again, as in the *Mirror for Magistrates*. But we are also invited to share a breathtaking secular perspective in which, identifying with Tamburlaine, we dare to seize control of Fortune's wheel. In doing so we find that even the medieval patterns take on a new transgressive texture. Popular drama, of course, had already tapped into the buried sadism of the *de casibus* trope. For all its jigging vein a play like *Cambises* provided a savage thrill and so probably did any medieval Crucifixion drama—the hidden, frightening glory all can feel in the humiliation of the great. But Marlowe confronted and expanded this material in his portrait of a legendary example of globe-striding *virtú,* keeping the scope and severity, the moral weight of medieval exempla, while adding the racy excitement of the kind of high-stakes amoral games of risk, speculation, and social mobility that only recently had begun to lick like flames at the minds of the London audience. The combination would have felt strangely illicit and empowering. The inclusion of Mycetes in *Tamburlaine* was a first step toward throwing open the borders that had kept a variety of feelings from mingling freely in the Elizabethan imagination— for convenience we can name them sadism, ambition, political curiosity, ethical intensity, moral ambiguity, but it would take a much longer study to tease them out in full. We shall want to return to this point—that tragedy in its great examples works by allowing us certain thrills ostensibly forbidden to it, a fact that tragic theory exists largely in order to conceal.

One of the most important ways in which dramatic genre functions is by advancing an illusion of origin, quite literally by dramatizing it. It makes us feel as if we were experiencing an instance of an already existing type but always as a departure from it, a complicated, deformed example of a category that was once more firmly and simply defined. *Hamlet* reads as a sophisticated expansion of revenge tragedy, but so does *The Spanish Tragedy,* the earliest extant example of the genre.

Did Greek tragedy *ever* consist simply of a dithyrambic chorus? It is interesting that every Greek play we possess seems repeatedly to refigure, in its intense oppositions, the "original" separation of dramatic chorus from dithyramb, individual from chorus, actor from actor. If Thespis didn't exist, tragedy would have had to invent him.

I used to think that film critics were incredibly sloppy when it came to tracing the development of film noir or even applying the term. Every example in their discussions seemed a little belated, a little contaminated by nongeneric elements; *Double Indemnity* or *Body and Soul* seemed as hybrid as *Chinatown*. Finally, it dawned: a film noir is any film that reminds us of certain films noir that never existed except as *this* film seems to derive from them. Of course, we also recognize family resemblances, as Alastair Fowler calls them, to films that do exist, and this, too, is an important aspect of genre. But family resemblance, especially as Wittgenstein and Fowler use the term, does not imply an idea of origin; it does not direct us to the purer traits of some supposed grandparent. None of the many Goldman faces I know is the equivalent of the ur-*Hamlet* or a tragedy by Thespis or the what-was-it-called a year or three before *Double Indemnity,* all ghostly back formations of the genre process. Admittedly, we sometimes misidentify an existing film or play as an ur-example, but we quickly find that *The Suppliant Women* or *The Spanish Tragedy* doesn't quite fill the bill; it's already varying the theme. And this, it turns out, is true of any genre you can name.

Both *Hamlet* and *The Spanish Tragedy* imply the existence of a set of generic rules from which they depart. They fill the stage with elaborations that are ostensibly excluded from the noirish, black-and-white, Seneca-by-lightning, witching time insistences of the "model" revenge tragedy. Nor is this sense of elaboration to be explained by the incorporation of Christian or other ethical worries about revenge ("Vengeance is mine, saith the Lord"). Even if, like many scholars, we choose to think of our model ur-package as including from the first a Christian moral, we still get a similar violation of the presumed original boundaries of the genre on precisely this ethical issue in every Elizabethan "revenge play" we meet. We can never quite lose—or keep—the Christian spin. In *Spanish Tragedy, Hamlet, Antonio's Revenge, 'Tis Pity,* there is always more room for thrills and doubt, for complication of whatever clear moral or emotional valence one thinks one can attach to the apparently simple purport of the haunting cry for revenge. For the madness that seems also to belong to the revenge play package is always in part a theatrical madness—an antic disposition that makes playacting of some sort always a destabilizing feature in the sweep of the hero-victim to his revenge.

In case the revenge play should appear too convenient an example of my principle, let me take an apparently more resistant case, the comedy of Molière, not *Don*

Juan or *Misanthrope* but the mainstream classics. The appearance of Alain and Georgette in scene 3 of *School for Wives* seems to signal a familiar Open Season on Foibles—and indeed seems to *re*signal it. Here is a pair of terminally incompetent servants, and isn't it just this attitude of observing and laughing at obvious flaws of character and perception that the sensible Chrysalde has already helped us take toward the hero, his friend Arnulphe, in the opening scene? But in fact the more scene 3 urges us to believe that this is what the play is up to, the more we become aware of a gap between Arnulphe's and his servants' foibles. Finally, it helps reinforce the sense that with Arnulphe we are in a different dimension of comic experience.

Molière's great obsessives like Arnulphe regularly emerge out of a deceptively familiar generic landscape. Little young lovers dance around the feet of these huge, crazed "blocking" figures. We are invited, indeed I would say we never can quite cease to believe, that we are cheerfully participating in a simple New Comedy triumph, lovers escaping from the toils of the older generation. But these clear and pleasant genre signals only help us to better hear the howls of an Arnulphe or Harpagon. (Not that New Comedy isn't itself always a bit newer than its "old" outlines always manage to suggest. Plautus, for example, is always taking advantage of the gaps that can be opened up by the spectacle of his troupe going to town on a Greek "original" on which his play is based. Much of the distinctive pleasure of Plautine comedy comes from watching popular commercial actors doing their version of what the Roman audience is thereby allowed to enjoy as comically old-fashioned or traditional. It's rather like listening to Fred Allen, Kenny Delmar, and Minerva Pious do *Carmen* on the old Texaco comedy hour.)

Modern drama will be considered in later sections, but here one might just remember the sound of the breaking string in *The Cherry Orchard* and how it breaks/enlarges generic assumptions. The power of this famous sound effect is not that it accomplishes a risky shift away from realism into some kind of fantasy but that (even more riskily) it enlarges the ambit of realism to contain something discontinuous, inexplicable, uncanny.

It is not only, then, that recognizable genre boundaries are often violated but that they seem to work dramatically *by* being violated, exactly to the extent and, in a sense, exactly at the point, that they are recognizable. ("*There's* the border, just passed, of old-fashioned revenge drama, comedy, tragedy, domestic drama, Noh of Ghosts." We have our keenest sense of *that* realm because we're in *this,* which seems different. But the country we thought we had left behind turns out to be bigger and stranger than expected.)

In any case, it will be critically revealing to watch such permeations. In the *Bacchae,* as we've seen, genre seems almost definitionally pure, uncontested, yet the figure who seems most to validate its uncontested clarities (this is drama, this is tragedy, this is the ritual as I, Dionysus, founder of tragedy, like it), most opens up the contradictions and confusions at the heart of the process. What is broached and breached at the climax of the *Bacchae* is not so much the genre of tragedy itself but what we might call the generic idea of tragedy, the idea of tragedy as a redeemingly serious subject for civic reflection, genre as a means toward soothing discursivity about a confusing art. The very voice that said *recognition—catharsis—social value* is now heard at the center of the arena, suddenly inflected with the mocking, boundless nastiness of Mr. Inside/Outside, Mr. Athenian Tragedy himself, in whose name real blood was shed before every performance.

Indeed, a similar kind of breaching runs across all Greek tragedy, even as an institution. Though Euripides' drama is usually singled out for its "self-conscious marking and manipulation of the conventions of tragedy," this self-conscious, ethically tense bending and stretching of the genre can be found everywhere in Greek tragedy, continually violating an implied norm. Civically, religiously, the exclusions are apparently absolute, iron-hard. Everything irreverent has ostensibly been banished to the animal bumptiousness of the satyr play. But all through Greek tragedy the shadow of the "old" animal chorus is plain, most of all in *Bacchae,* whose choruses bristle with invitations to imitate the movement of animals. Also the very sharp intertexture, in all the tragedies, of highly conventionalized elements with realism and idiosyncratic treatment suggests the regular breaking of a contract of exclusion, a contrast of modes that seems itself conventional. The juxtaposition, for example, of stichomythia with choral ode adds to the tragic contest the sense of a contest of types, a generic tension that would seem to echo the clash of traditional and emergent social values Vernant finds characteristic of the Athenian "tragic moment."

Probably the contest itself, with its apparently invariant procedures yet remarkably original achievements, enacted a tension between rules and freedom, community and the individual, benign civic celebration of the god and terrifying individual appropriations of godhead. *Antigone* begins by excluding the cautious norm-minded sister in the name of a kind of transgressive theatricalism, an identification on the heroine's part with both the gods and the dead. Antigone wins our attention and her play the civic prize, but she destroys her city. The Oedipus who initiates his play's tragic ritual in the actorlike role of priestly healer is, of course, sicker than his subjects, who cluster like an audience around him:

Sick as you are, none is more sick than I.

This line invites us to read the Oedipus-actor's mask in two conflicting ways, the second of which undermines the first: (1) the divinely healthy leader condescending to play the role of sick man for the benefit of society; (2) the hopelessly contaminated man blindly undertaking the part of invulnerable leader. The idea of tragic performance as a kind of civic medicine feels very dubious here. In the end neither *Antigone* nor *Oedipus* is any more devoted to healing than the *Bacchae*.

Here we come upon a larger point about tragedy and our identifications. One notable witness to the horrors of our century has written:

We have to become murderers in order to experience ourselves as real.

Though this statement occurs in a novel set in Europe during and shortly after the Second World War, I don't think we are meant to take it simply as the narrow description of a modern era numbed by a reality it cannot assimilate. It hints at an aspect of tragedy that is usually suppressed in critical discussions but to my mind defines the genre. Traditionally, our reflections about tragedy allow us to see ourselves as *victims*. From Aristotle on, all the bad stuff in these plays is interpreted as not our fault; instead, it is taken as a terrifying example of what life makes us face. Yes, the tragic hero may be understood to represent us, but only up to a point; a subtle distancing is always implied. The experience of tragedy is carefully parsed as experience of ourselves not quite *as* ourselves but as forced into the company of murderers, of ourselves seeing a version of ourselves with a twist (a *hamartia*) that makes us alien, but ultimately of ourselves as a good audience, kink free and publicly acceptable—wondering, sensitive, battle-tested pillars of the community. In this view tragic experience is something we have to *get through,* racked by all too human fear and sympathy, sharing the heroes' suffering and courage, on the way to manifesting our own heroic selves, ourselves as better-than-gods. But tragic heroes, without exception, invite us, quite simply, to *become murderers*. We half-admit to it in certain special cases, cases we can more easily pretend to be distanced from. So we acknowledge that Macbeth is a murderer, a traitor, a paranoid, and daintily point out that this is the interesting rare example of a tragedy about an *evil man*—though really he's not that much more of a wild beast (and no less appealing to us) than Romeo or Bussy d'Ambois when they're in the vein. And, of course, when the hero is a woman . . . oh my, what a *monster* Hedda is! But like the rest, like even Brutus or Antigone in their Sunday best, these tragic heroes thrill us because their plays allow us to become killers like them.

What a triumphant, blazing speech we get when Oedipus takes us through his encounter with the insufferable Laius and his officious men at the crossroads. Oedipus' narrative pulses with all the athletic, daring, contagious mettle of his youth, right up to the climax, "And then . . . I killed them all!" The pleasure of this wonderful moment is not much mentioned in the critical literature, a silence that speaks volumes about the secret operations of genre.

IV

For all the well-known differences between stage and screen as media, I know of no more brilliant contemporary meditation on dramatic genre than Almodóvar's movie *Kika*. In its provocative and frequently startling deployment of generic adjustments and boundaries, it opens up large perspectives on the subject, to an extent unparalleled in any recent play or film. For me it both refines and drives home the relevance of the view of genre developed in the previous section.

Kika begins with two sequences, a photographer snapping models in their underwear in sexy poses and a young man driving through the countryside in a sports car. Neither motif is very original, though both are freshly elegant and slightly exaggerated. Then the young man arrives home and finds his mother very realistically dead, a suicide, lots of thick dark blood about. Cut to a caption, "Three years later," and then to an amusing training session for upscale cosmeticians, full of practical advice. The suicide sequence clearly tests the generic signals, which are not all that clear at first until the bloody realism points a contrast in retrospect; then they become very clear in the playfulness of the sudden narrative jump and the beauty school pleasantries that follow. The mother's death and the blood seem embedded in the comedy but not quite contained.

I've suggested that, if genre, at least in drama, seems

to be about what gets excluded and, as it were, excluded in advance, it may be even more accurate to say that it's about how certain things apparently destructive to the performance actually get included as we go along. Almodóvar seems wonderfully aware of this, and the problem of inclusion and threat is focused in the bodily fluids that, embarrassingly, keep appearing in *Kika,* always at moments when generic containment seems threatened—not only blood (frequently) but sweat, semen, and vomit. One thinks unavoidably of AIDS, and, brilliantly, AIDS is alluded to at a point in the picture that marks its most extreme testing of the boundaries of genre and taste, alluded to just enough to heighten our new, appalled contemporary sensitivity to the play of bodily fluids as threatening to eroticism. (In *Kika* Almodóvar makes one pungently aware of the sensual loss involved in forbidding the exchange of fluids—just as these fluids are usually banished from the voyeuristic pleasures of film and fashion photography. In the opening sequence we see an assistant dabbing tissues under the arms of the model between snaps.) Kika is a cosmetician, and the movie regularly draws attention to cosmetic codes both in life and art, to what they exclude and to their violation. Kika and her boyfriend meet cute when she is invited to make up a corpse; we are shown underarm hair in unexpected situations.

After a prolonged and deliberately wacky rape scene, in which a "comically" extended discussion of condoms (not used) between rapist and victim heightens our anxiety about the contrast between the "seriousness" of what is going on and what we're ostensibly being asked to feel—anxiety, that is, about genre—after this scene is apparently over, and the rapist, about to come for the third time, is chased by the police to the balcony of a posh Madrid apartment, his semen, so far only implied, suddenly appears, falling from several stories on the upturned face of a female inquiring reporter (the ultimate reaction shot), and making a trace that copies the cosmetically enhanced blood-red scar on the other side of her nose, a self-inflicted wound, which has earned her the name "Scarface." Is this funny, is this possibly funny? It's an "Is this funny, is this possibly funny?" moment. The droplet is, as it were, embedded but not contained in the comedy, and the treatment makes us feel the process by which genre includes by seeming exclusion, makes us feel both the problem and excitement of it.

The inquiring reporter—the sexy Victoria Abril—is a popular TV star (a *therapist* turned TV star), whose favorite costume is that of a walking camera, a kind of black leather wetsuit with an emphatically phallic, long, narrow camera swiveling on her helmeted head. She wears many costumes, all pornographic. But the mockery of therapy and sex serves somehow only to raise the film's psychological and sexual stakes. Psychobabble in *Kika* often functions as a comic marker, but the jargon-filled explanations, offered in scenes that deliberately remind us of soap opera, often turn out actually to improve our understanding of the characters.

Death seems important to the idea of genre. One thinks of drama's most famous emblem, the laughing and weeping masks of comedy and tragedy, and life and death seem to be the obvious distinction between the two genres. Comedy, it would appear, cannot include death, and tragedy must include it. We know, of course, that neither statement is true, but comedy and tragedy *seem* that way, and that's the way of genre. From the opening suicide to the meeting over a corpse to the long search for a serial killer that runs through the film to the heroine's final flight from a family that seems almost ludicrously overburdened by murder, suicide, fatal accident, and a peculiar form of narcolepsy, death is apparently the big issue in *Kika*. But the real question genre raises may be the one that seems finally to be the truly big issue in *Kika*—the question of liking to fuck and where that places us with relation to the ethical and ontological real. Kika likes to fuck, and that makes her the heroine of the movie. (The rapist's sister, describing her brother's youth, says, "Like all abnormals, he liked to fuck," to which Kika replies, "Not only abnormals.") Kika is the cosmetician with a heart of gold and as such, and like many of the women in the movie, a big ethical question mark right out of the contemporary problematic of film, so familiar an inhabitant of pornotopia, so much an ideological support for the voyeurism and male-dominated fantasy that, we are often warned, is generic or threatens to be generic to film. Almodóvar's movie appeals frequently and successfully to the male gaze while reminding us just how dubious this appeal is.

Liking to fuck is a kind of bottom-line version not only of the comic impulse but of artistic pleasure, too, especially the bodily pleasures of theater and the movies. There's no doubt that *Kika* retains an allegiance to the comic impulse, just as it does to the idea of Kika's basic good sense and decency. In the universe of this film Kika's instincts are healthy. But all the generic doublings and dubieties keep the issue of health—especially the health of our appetites as sex and movie lovers—on a knife edge.

In *Kika* the number of characters making questionable use of sex, violence, and images of women for purposes of self-gratification is large. The therapist-reporter specializes in stories of rape. The main romantic hero is both photographer and voyeur. His stepfather (and main romantic rival) is a writer and serial killer, who is writing a novel in which his crimes are reproduced, disguised as the work of a lesbian, who becomes the novel's first-person narrator. It is suggested, too, that the therapist–TV reporter is a lesbian, but I think this is intended largely to link her function as a character in Almodóvar's film—she discovers the murderer's identity through her specialty of filming sex crimes—to the function of the lesbian murderer in the serial killer's novel. Through her Almodóvar is able to figure himself as behaving in a manner that parallels the murderer's. That is, as imagining his own (artistic) crimes against women as acts of *female* sexual perversion.

One could argue that Almodóvar is in bad faith here, allowing himself to get away with his own sexist fantasies. Similarly, males in the audience (or the audience as male) may seem allowed to savor the murderer's stalking/savoring in the guise of moral correctness. But the movie is so aware of how the management of genre, of systems of exclusion, allows one to get, not only away with it but out of it and into it, that these pornographic maneuvers seem yet a further instance of genre bending on the filmmaker's part. Almodóvar's awareness of the strange slides and shifts of position from which we enter or pursue our fantasies gives *Kika* its own healthy energy. But his wise and playful understanding of the honest turmoil of our sexual lives is inseparable from his appreciation of the seductive ways of genre. Both the limits of genre and its powers, the hopes, fears, and imperfectly defended pleasures that genre institutes, are thrillingly involved in this movie.

Genre, it appears, doesn't so much keep out the viruses that threaten a play (with mirth in funeral, for example) as enable the play to digest them. Genre in drama most effectively enlarges the area of pleasure by *imperfectly* defending the area. The trick is to make the defense imperfect while not breaking the process down. Polonius' ludicrous riff on genre elaborates a tremor initiated as early in *Hamlet* as Claudius' reference to "mirth in funeral, and . . . dirge in marriage"—a mingling of genres unacceptable to Hamlet in his insistently tragic garb, the "inky cloak" that he nevertheless insists is in no way theatrical. Four acts later the clowns' mirth at Ophelia's funeral works not as a (perfectly conventional) piece of clownery in what is apparently a familiar

Elizabethan mode, the illusory generic clarity of "comic relief." Instead, it expands the ambit of tragedy, helping Hamlet become intimate with a skull and thus opening an abyss beneath any conventionally "tragic," crocodile-eating treatment of death.

V

I'm suggesting, then, that we think of dramatic genre as part of a system of permeabilities, porous, flexible boundaries like the walls of a living cell, that admit, express, extend, and to a degree overcome the basic permeability anxieties of dramatic performance. From the point of view of contemporary philosophy, the most interesting of these permeabilities may be the mutual permeability of actor and script, because it addresses our more-than-philosophical anxiety about the relation between persons and texts. The popular poststructuralist view, of course, is that there is nothing that is not writing, nothing available to human understanding that is not a text, a semiotic system. This view is crucially challenged by the phenomenon of theatrical performance, particularly by what we normally and perhaps misleadingly call subtext.

If subtexts were in fact reducible to texts, there would be no need for actors. Acting would simply provide a text supplementary to the script. Now, of course, actors do provide this; all acting does. But, if subtext were *only* a text, only another kind of writing, it could be kind of written—published in books or perhaps made the subject of essays on drama—and there would be no need for the theater, for performance, except as an aid to lazy readers. Theater would be a way of underlining or explaining the script, providing a sensual reward to compel attention—a pauper's bible indeed.

Such a view ignores a defining feature of dramatic performance, which may be called the actor's entry into the text. Certainly, it is possible to treat an actor's performance semiotically—and, of course, there are many signs, many kinds of writing, associated with acting and theatrical production. But in drama one finds inevitably an element in excess of what can be semiotically extracted—something that is also neither irrelevant to nor, in appropriately excellent examples, completely independent of the text. No matter how exhaustively one tries to translate what an actor does with a script into a kind of writeable commentary on it, there will always also remain the *doing* of it—the bodily life of the actor moving into the world, at a specific moment in time, to set in motion these words, these gestures, these writeable ideas, this other identity. And, if the doing were itself to be reduced to a text, there would still remain the doing of the doing. The actor enters the text. She brings her full bodily life to bear on the script that she is playing—and great scripts both demand and greatly reward that full focus.

Now this is certainly part of the private reading process too—one reader reading alone is also entering a text. But the theatrical process more urgently and complexly insists on this fact, on its pathos, its problematics, its physical base, its link to the horror, boredom, and glory of daily life. Indeed, this is one of the places where it's especially interesting to imagine the theatrical model of textual encounter as primary instead of derivative from literature. If we reverse the ingrained habit and think of literature as a specialization of drama rather than the other way around, we may be able to advance beyond some celebrated impasses in the theory of literature.

For instance, this view corrects, perhaps actually dissolves, the impasse that poststructuralism seems to have arrived at in the question of human presence and textuality. Like a script, any text is by definition not just a field of meanings but a field for entry. Studded with signs of entry, calling out for entry, it shades off into a field of nontext that it cannot do without. Contrary to Derrida, there is *always* an hors-texte, a place from which someone at some moment needs to enter, even to constitute the text as a text. And drama insists on the problems and poignancies of this circumstance, this mutually constitutive commerce between that which is writing and that which is not.

A quotation from Wittgenstein is suggestive here, since it seems to echo the notion that texts, as texts, require something like a dramatic entry:

> The conclusion which one draws . . . is that what must be added to the dead signs in order to make a live proposition is something immaterial, with properties different from all mere signs.

Any theatrical performance foregrounds this semiotic insufficiency of texts, as indeed does any script, by calling out for an actor.

The relation between actor and text and between text and performance is easily obscured by the physical fact that scripts are normally written out—usually printed out—and given to the actors before they begin to rehearse. Thus text may logically seem to enjoy an existence prior to performance. But, when a playwright composes a line, she is attempting to imagine something an actor might say in an effective performance. The actual utterance will not take place until actor and line come together in a theatrical moment. The published script itself might just as well be prepared afterward and attempt to describe the theatrical moment retrospectively. This is in fact the case with most published movie scripts.

Imagine that *Hamlet* developed out of a series of improvisations, with Shakespeare first taking the title role and then all the other roles in turn, culling the best bits, stringing them together, and only then putting them on paper. There's no logical reason why the script produced in this fashion should be any different from the one that we imagine Shakespeare to have written by candlelight after days of solitary thought. A play may arguably be the product of its author's imagination, but a play is not the product of its script; the script is merely that part of a play that gets written down. Why do actors long to be "off book"? They know that, as long as script is prior to performance, the play does not properly exist. Memorizing a part is actually a means of freeing oneself from its mere textuality.

The point is that, in the theater, text and performance are experienced as generating one another. To think of the text of *Hamlet* as the little Penguin edition stuffed in the actor's back pocket while he rehearses is to distort the phenomena of performance. The distortion is reinforced by our experience of literature, where the physical stability of books seductively suggests that the texts we enter when we open them are similarly solid and unchanging.

In the theater we're always aware of two things: that the actors are acting and that they're acting *something*. The "text" is being produced by the actors, but it is also producing what the actors do. Even if it's an improvisation, we feel that it is an improvisation of something—a plan we experience as behind the performance but also as emerging now. This in turn casts light on the oddly embarrassing question, somehow vulgar but never quite suppressible, of whether it's best to see a play without having read it—whether when we see it we should try to forget having read it, whether that would be an affectation, whether it is possible, whether it matters. The preferred way of dealing with the question, certainly made easier by our current preference for belatedness, is to treat it as hopelessly naive. Of course, one says, the experience of a play is dependent on some text or other. Every moment in life is textual, isn't it? Why pretend otherwise? But the correct answer is a little more complex and rather more specific to theater. In the theater, after all, a certain kind of pretending is fundamental—as is an awareness of script and improvisation, of text and performance, as mutually present. The mutuality affects the kind of pretending we do, the part we play as audience. We pretend that what the actors are doing is spontaneous in order to relish the script, but in order to relish their performance we must know that we're pretending. Our appreciation depends on our knowing it's *not* spontaneous. We pretend not to know the script in order to enjoy its unfolding, but in order to enjoy it fully we must also know that it's a script. We play the part of a surprised audience. We respond to the play as if we had never seen it before—even if we *have* never seen it before. We watch any play as if for the first time, *even* the first time.

But, though theatrical performance gives textuality a distinctive and revealing spin, the mutually constitutive relation of actor and text has a cultural importance that extends well beyond the theater. The phenomenon of the unwriteable, text-constituting entry from outside the text is inseparable from the phenomenon of writing itself. Text ridden, language imprisoned as our lives may be, it is a catastrophic mistake to think of text and language as somehow logically prior to our existence. We constitute both text and language every time we speak or read or write. Where, my friend, is the textuality of *this* moment—with the sun and the trees and the century outside? Certainly, a text is part of it. I am producing the text, and you are producing it—no doubt out of many old and insidious textual fragments, but still we are producing it at this moment, producing two texts in fact, two separate incommensurable infinite ranges of text, bridged by this little piece of text that lies between us, over which we may struggle for a moment, linked only by our differing, mutually responsive tugs, until you decide to let go. The text of our own brief *Hamlet* is the readable, vanishing, endlessly arguable trace of what we just *did*—the double entry that made the dead signs live.

We might think here of Krapp in Beckett's play, surrounded by a proliferating supply of texts (tapes) into which he feels compelled to enter and reenter. His entries are often subtextual, in that they respond to and inflect the earlier texts, but they too are recorded and become texts for later comment. Krapp performs his play against the text of his tapes. He himself seems threatened and diminished by the process, always placed and reduced again by being "taped" (as we say), pathetic in his attempt to make contact with an always receding "life" by means of these mechanical representations. Yet by his interventions, even his silences, he always introduces a residue, a further response, a bit of new life that the tapes do not exhaust, though by doing so he also performs the pathos of attempting to invest this residue with meaning.

Just as in the script of this or any play, there is, among the specified lines and gestures, always a space where the actor is required to enter, where he must *say* and *act* the lines, bring his full bodily life to bear upon them, so the life of Krapp's play lies in his movement among his texts and intertexts, his entry that, though sadly belated and predictable, must inescapably be made *now,* into the tapes and taped commentaries, the texts that define and mock him. This inescapable minimum of present focus, Krapp's quantum of entry, brings us close to the heart of Beckett's enterprise.

Too often we talk about Beckett as if his plays were simple exercises in mockery, demolitions of a pitiful human pretension to meaning. If this were true, *Krapp's Last Tape* would be a rather tedious example of overkill. Here is a man who has been foolish enough (repeatedly) to think that life means something, now seeing how meaningless it's all repeatedly been. Can't we just lie back and accept this fundamental absurdity? But as mortals, as beings who are forced to live in time, we are constantly compelled to enter a particular mortal moment. We cannot help making a mark on the texts we enter, and, feeble and pathetic as our mark may be, it works like meaning.

This, I think, suggests the color of Beckett's existentialism—to be stuck in being is to be stuck in meaning. The famous exchange between Didi and Gogo, "This is becoming really insignificant.—Not enough!" is misread if we take it simply as a blow at our pretensions to meaning, that is, that we can't begin to say how absurd existence is. The fact is, it also strikes at our equally absurd pretensions to meaninglessness. While we exist, there is always a human space, this mud for instance, where meaning goes on being manufactured, a space for entry. (As Molloy, flat on his face in the muck, cries with surprise, "Christ, there's crawling!") Of course, to be really meaningful, the meaning must be true to reality, that is, really insignificant; it has to be minimal. And it's never minimal, never insignificant enough.

Over and over Krapp enters his texts:

> *He suddenly bends over machine, switches off, wrenches off tape, throws it away, puts on the other, winds it forward to the passage he wants, switches on, listens staring front . . . Krapp's lips move.*
>
> TAPE: . . . Perhaps my best years are gone. When there was a chance of happiness. But I wouldn't want them back. Not with the fire in me now.

"The fire in me now" is simultaneously (1) a laughable pretension to significance and (2) a version of the sub-text-that-is-other-than-text, the (however feeble) flame that inhabits any utterance, the present entry that makes drama out of what Krapp is listening to. Between the individual and the crap he deposits, between Krapp and his tapes, lies the play's action.

Even Beckett's title plays with this impossible/minimal persistence of meaning, using its generic familiarity as a form of genre disturbance. From the start, and even before the start, the title is a sign of what (among other things as a "Beckett play") we know this play can't possibly be. What is Krapp's Last Tape? X's Last Y, like Trent's Last Case or Custer's Last Stand, suggests finality. But Krapp's Last Tape is last year's tape, merely one in a sequence. It is also the unfinished tape that is being made now. And it is what this tape will become once it is finished, a textual object, a script for further entry.

This is also what this play will become once it has been constituted by this performance—a text to be brought to life by an actor's performance tomorrow, as each tape is annually brought to life by Krapp. The text has its being in its invitations and responses to entry.

Throughout his work Beckett is concerned with the minimal seepages between person and text, with the sensation of a contact beyond the boundaries of representation—not only minimal but under the least promising of conditions. The actors in *Ohio Impromptu* enter their text at a point between text and loss, on a kind of hinge between them. There is a literal text in the play, a text about loss, that is read, reread, and listened to—and a reader and a listener dressed identically:

> *L [Listener] seated at table facing front towards end of long side audience right. Bowed head propped on right hand. Face hidden. Left hand on table. Long black coat. Long white hair.*
>
> *R [Reader] seated at table in profile centre of short side audience right. Bowed head propped on right hand. Left hand on table. Book on table before him open at last pages. Long black coat. Long white hair.*

These figures resemble not only each other but the subject of the text, a man defined by irremediable loss. Like the man described in the text, the Listener seems to be drawn to the text because of his loss, a loss the text describes. The play of identities or identifications (one cannot be sure where one leaves off and the other begins

in *Ohio Impromptu*), like the pairing of reader and listener, reminds one, seems to draw on and heighten our
sense of, the divided selves of drama—actor and audience, script and performance, inside and out.

When the Listener in *Ohio Impromptu* wishes to have a
sentence read a second time, he knocks on the table that
joins and divides Listener and Reader. The knocking of
the Listener and the Reader's obedient return to the previous sentence may well remind us of the cliché about
literature as opposed to drama; the reader of a book can
always stop the process, we are told, go back and reread.
But, of course, he can't *always* do so. One doesn't read,
any more than one lives, in infinite time. We enter into
the texts we read, as into everything in our lives, as part
of the tight drama of ending, of losing, the painful
endgame to which Beckett is so sensitive. In this play, as
we shall see, the Listener's final effort at entering the
Reader's text carries with it a strong sensation that
boundaries have been crossed. The knocking suddenly
fails to work, and the Listener very dramatically discovers that the reading is over.

Do we care about *Ohio Impromptu*'s genre, at least in
the sense that students of genre understand the question?
One answer suggests some practical advice for genre-
minded critics. Instead of anything so sharply determina-
tive as we normally expect (or think we expect) of
genre, we may, in responding to the play, simply recognize an attitude or mood being solicited from the audience, a response that draws on expectations familiar to
us from various corners of modern drama. Historically,

the mood of *Ohio Impromptu* may have something to do with Strindbergian hypnotism, with Wagner, with "art" performance in general, especially with art performance in the style of Yeats's Noh-influenced later plays. These, and perhaps familiarity with earlier Beckett plays, are enough to direct our attention and expectation in the best way for the play to unfold to advantage. And here is where the practical point for genre studies lies. Loose bundles of expectation may often be more to the purpose than any precisely identifiable system of signals. We know the *kind* of thing we are watching, and that means a readiness for certain moods and rhythms.

In *Ohio Impromptu,* for instance, when the Listener discovers that the reading is at an end, there's a moment or passage of final recognition, which is as much a recognition of genre as anything—as much, that is, a recognition of what kind of experience we're having as of what the characters are achieving or what the situation represented is or signifies. It comes at the very end of the play, as the dramaturgy and the language become most Yeatsian:

> READER: So the sad tale a last time told they sat on as
> though turned to stone. Through the single window
> dawn shed no light. From the street no sound of
> reawakening. Or was it that buried in who knows
> what thoughts they paid no heed? To light of day.
> To sound of reawakening. What thoughts who
> knows. Thoughts, no, not thoughts. Profounds of
> mind. Buried in who knows what profounds of
> mind. Of mindlessness. Whither no light can reach.

No sound. So sat on as though turned to stone. The
sad tale a last time told.
Pause.
Nothing is left to tell.
Pause. R makes to close book.
Knock. Book half-closed.
Nothing is left to tell.
Pause. R closes book.
Knock.
Silence. Five seconds.
Simultaneously they lower their right hands to table, raise
their heads and look at each other. Unblinking. Expres-
sionless.
Ten seconds.
Fade out.

It is in the stillness, the persistence of the final image,
that the climax comes, as in the Yeatsian dance. And in
its reference to "profounds of mind," the language that
prepares the climax echoes Yeats on the Noh drama.
When he talks in "Certain Noble Plays of Japan" about
the Japanese dancer in performance, Yeats says the
dancer is able to inhabit "a deep of the mind," and he
repeats the phrase three times in a half-page.

Beckett's play ends, as it foretold/retold, in "silence"
where "no light can reach" and only after an uncannily
still moment, long extended in theater time, in which
the eyes of Listener and Reader meet. Is that a recognition? It is a moment, for us, of heightened awareness,
whether of mind or mindlessness we cannot know——a

moment of private absence and separation, which yet owes everything to the mutualities of public performance, of bodies projected into texts and texts into bodies. A moment achingly private, somehow impossibly stilled and fixed and made transpersonal. A moment in which boundaries are permeated and rendered impassable at the same time.

VI

One reason a good acting performance is appealing is because it overcomes in a striking way a threat of awkwardness that menaces any attempt at self-presentation in ordinary life. Getting up before an audience, remembering one's lines yet appearing natural and spontaneous, simultaneously managing to function as someone remembered from the past and a convincing version of oneself in the present—these are heightened instances of difficulties we all can appreciate. Just as theatrical genre allows us to slide across boundaries of experience that appear unbreachable, so the smoothly operating skills of an actor allow him to negotiate the apparently irreconcilable realms of script and performance, writing and doing, present and past. The smoothness is itself worth thinking about, a clue to the cultural power of drama.

The key to this aspect of performance is what the anthropologist Victor Turner calls *flow*, a term he borrows from the theory of play. This is a phenomenon necessary to much of the functioning of daily life. In ordinary behavior we experience flow in the seamless transitions and transactions of social exchange:

> Flow denotes the holistic sensation present when we act with total involvement [and is] a state in which action follows action according to an internal logic which seems to need no conscious intervention

on our part . . . we experience it as a unified flowing from one moment to the next, in which we feel in control of our actions, and in which there is little distinction between self and environment; between stimulus and response; or between past, present and future.

Flow depends on a movement across boundaries, which if acknowledged would make the process impossible. Not that an awareness of boundaries entirely ceases during passages of flow, but it recedes as the result of some kind of centering focus. As Turner puts it, illustrating his point by a theatrical example:

There is no dualism in "flow"; while an actor may be aware of what he is doing, he cannot be aware that he is aware—if he does, there is a rhythmic behavioral or cognitive break. Self-consciousness makes him stumble.

The centering focus I referred to, what Turner's sources call "total involvement," may remind us of what I described earlier as the source of subtext—the actor's focusing of his full bodily life upon the text at a moment in time. At carnival and at other moments of intense communal activity, we have a heightened sense of flow, as barriers dissolve between individuals, between modes of behavior, between public and private presentations and conceptions of the self. For most of us flow is harder to achieve in theatrical performance than in ordinary life; the ability to achieve flow onstage before an audience is a mark of the talented performer. In the theater we see and experience flow as part of the actors' performance and to some extent as part of our own reactions. We are aware of it as making seamless the relations between past and present, intention and act, character and actor, mind and body, script and performance, between a set of already prescribed indications and the spontaneity of an unfolding event.

Both our impression of a coherent self-identity and our conviction that we can find and convey meaning in our exchanges with the world depend on the phenomenon of flow. In ordinary life serious disruptions of flow are accompanied by breakdowns of psychic and linguistic coherence. At least one important modern play, Peter Handke's *The Ride across Lake Constance,* uses such disruptions of flow as part of its basic strategy. Interestingly, this is a work of extremely problematic genre, problematic even at the level of drama-as-genre.

The Ride across Lake Constance is plainly concerned with questioning—one could legitimately say deconstructing—the modes of signification that language makes available to us, while at the same time undermining the apparent coherence of theatrical performance. And it does so by severely testing the phenomenon of flow. Handke's title refers to the German legend of a horseman who, having galloped across Lake Constance on the ice, learns that his feat should have been impossible because the ice on the lake is only an inch thick. Upon hearing this, he collapses, falls from his horse, and dies.

For Handke all communication is just such an impossible journey, one we take every day across the thin ice of language.

Throughout the play there is a felt danger of collapsing into dissociation. In the following scene Bergner, a "beautiful" woman who seems to alternate between the roles of femme fatale and woman-as-victim, tries to comb her hair. Handke builds here on a familiar disorientation, one that often affects people when they try to coordinate their actions with a mirror image. At such a moment one may become aware what a complex process of "reading" supports the simple movements of daily life, the flow on which self-coherence depends:

> Bergner *is combing herself, but with movements becoming increasingly more insecure. She does not know in which direction to comb while viewing herself in the mirror. With a small pair of scissors she wants to cut a strand of hair, holding it away from her head, but keeps missing until she finally lets go of the strand. She wants to put on makeup, pencils the eyebrows and the eyelines, puts rouge on her cheeks, powders her nose, puts on lipstick. But as she does this her movements become more and more shaky, and contradictory. She confuses the direction in which she wishes to draw the lines. She is mixed up. She wants to put the cosmetics back into the handbag but they fall to the floor. She walks away. She turns around, walks in the opposite direction, at the same time looking back over her shoulder, turns around again. She is totally confused, her face is badly made up. She walks in a direction where no one is and says:*

> *"Help me!" but with wrong gestures, hopping around. She bumps into things, bends forward to pick up things that physically lie behind her.*

Bergner here looks like a poster girl for postmodernism.

At moments of broken flow one is threatened not by the absence of meaning but by the overwhelming anarchy of possible meanings. The successful "ride" that our language games normally accomplish works by damping down and stabilizing this ominous, boundary-less flood of significations. As Handke's play progresses, we become aware that we live our lives in the grip of arbitrary conventions of meaning and that we remain comfortable and safe by staying within these conventions and the power relations (including sexual relations) built up by them. Whenever we become estranged from them, when the arbitrariness becomes apparent, flow breaks down and anguish results.

Among the generic breachings and confusions Handke introduces into *Ride,* there occurs a typically modern confusion as to genre, so typical that it might be considered a modern dramatic genre itself—tragedy undermined by irony, comedy painfully grotesque. This is the kind of mixture we find Shaw praising in *The Wild Duck* (while rather simplifying the effect of the mix):

> To look on with horror and pity at a profound tragedy, shaking with laughter all the time at an irresistible comedy: that is what The Wild Duck was like last Monday at the Globe.

Wild Duck is not the first play to combine such feelings in a way that goes beyond the shifts and alternations of classical drama. We may already recognize a subversive mingling or undermining of genres in Büchner and even Kleist. And certainly the comedy and irony of Ibsen's earlier *Doll's House* and *Ghosts* take their toll on their heroines' tragic intensities. But with *Wild Duck* we are involved from the start with feelings that are radically at odds and meant to remain so. Just when things get most sacrificial they turn smirky; the funniest posture brings on the most pain. We are not dealing here simply with the general tendency of genre to absorb what it pretends to exclude. This is not the modulation-through-dissonance of a Malvolio nor the tonal variety of a *Winter's Tale*. It's a particular genre-antagonistic edge, which we feel with just the illusion of comprehensiveness, of familiarity, that is typical of genre—and we feel it in typical modern plays from *The Seagull* to *The Balcony* to Pirandello's *Henry IV*.

Plays of this genre often issue in a very distinctive type of climax, apparently also invented by Ibsen, which is itself almost a signature of modern drama. In this type of climax a conclusive gesture is reduced by its context to inconclusiveness, a long developing positive drive is vitiated by doubt, a project of enlightenment gutters into absence like a candle flame flaring and going out. In such plays we are usually caught up in the campaign of the individual soul to break through to reality in what the soul perceives to be an unreal world, a campaign on the side of joy, of inner flowering, a campaign that seems to be leading to a breakthrough. And then comes the moment of breakthrough, in which the campaigning soul wakes up to—absence, irony, radical limitation. In the nineteenth century this is usually represented as an absence of joy, of fulfilled life. Later dramatists tend to treat it as an absence of reality. But, whether it be Mrs. Alving discovering, as dawn spectacularly breaks, that the joy of life is impossible or the revolutionaries in *The Balcony* learning that their war against illusion can only be sustained by illusion or Brecht's Shen Te finding that she can only be a good woman by masquerading as a bad man, the final revelation opens a fissure between the individual drive that makes for the play's action and the world in which the individual self tries to act.

At the end of *Ride* we get a climactic recognition that is both a parody of dramatic recognition in general and a particularly haunting, emptied-out version of this generic modern climax. It is a long sequence that needs to be quoted in full, in whose final beat darkness replaces the beginning of a smile.

The sequence begins with a stage direction, "[The characters] all hunch up more and more." In the play's vocabulary (as in Ibsen's) the hunching is a sign of lost flow. The child's noisy crying at the beginning of the scene picks up an agitation that all the actors seem to feel at this point as their projects of smooth social exchange grind to a halt in an atmosphere of bullying and school-yard torment. The Woman with the Scarf who emerges from the wings has also appeared at the beginning of the play, vacuuming the set and setting the play in motion by removing the drop cloths that cover the furniture and one of the characters. By bringing on the child, she initiates the play's last, fragmented moments, punctuated by the child's cries and sudden silences:

They all hunch up more and more. Now one hears a noise emanating from backstage, a high-pitched, pathetic howling.

The howling coincides with a slight darkening onstage. Porten *immediately stops and hunches up too.*

The Woman *with the* Scarf *steps swiftly out of the wings and walks to the second tapestry door without looking at anyone. As soon as she opens the door, there is quiet behind it. Instead one hears the rustling of a newspaper, which is lying just inside the door. The* Woman *goes inside and returns with a big* Doll *that represents a* Child. *The* Child *is quiet now, it has the hiccups. It is wearing a gold-embroidered white nightgown and looks very true to life. The mouth is enormous and open. As the* Woman *reaches center stage with the* Child, *it starts to bawl terribly, somehow without any preliminaries.* George, *jacket over his head, quickly leaps toward the chest and closes the drawer. The bawling stops at once.*

The Woman *carries the* Child *now from one to the other very fast, and in passing, during brief stops, it reaches for the women's breasts and between the men's legs. Very rapidly it also wipes off all the things that had been lying on the table, then pulls away the lace tablecloth and drops it. When the* Woman *stands with the* Child *beside* Bergner, *who seems to be still asleep, it begins to bawl again, and as suddenly as if it had never stopped. The*

Woman *holds it in such a way the* Child *sees* Bergner *from the front. It stops bawling at once and is carried away.*

The Woman *returns alone, closes the tapestry door, and goes off. After she has gone, they all sit there motionless. One of them tries to reach for something, but stops as soon as he starts. Someone else tries a gesture that atrophies instantly. A third wants to reply with a gesture, interrupts it twitching. They squat there, start to do something simultaneously; one or two of them even open their mouths—a few sounds, then all of them grow stiff and cuddle up, make themselves very small as if freezing to death.*

Only Bergner *sits there the whole time motionless, with eyes closed. All of a sudden, as though she were playing "waking up," she moves slightly. By and by, the others look toward her.* Von Stroheim *gets up and bends down to her. She again moves a little. The others are motionless. She opens her eyes and recognizes* Von Stroheim; *she begins to smile.*

The stage becomes dark.

The child gives us a feeling of the primary, of that which is prior to language. The moment of face-to-face behavior with Bergner produces the "recognition" of a face that the infant cannot possibly recognize but which calms him, as indeed the sight of a face can calm a child, and thus ends the tragic threat of the "high-pitched pathetic howling." At this point we may be likely to feel that something is being resolved, that the play has won through to some basic soothing ground of relationship. But flow breaks down once more, and now the actors seem to be "freezing to death."

At the very end Bergner, who suddenly acts "as though she were playing 'waking up'" and then "begins" to smile at Von Stroheim, appears to be navigating us toward something more positive, but everything we have seen of her relationship with Von Stroheim (and with language, playacting, and sexuality) undermines the positive valence of her gestures. Darkness, which has been falling since the child's first howls, obliterates her never-completed smile. The conclusion is made to feel additionally conclusive by incorporating many details the audience has encountered earlier in the play (the rustling newspaper, the games of association, as between the shutting of the drawer and the shutting up of the child), particularly verbal details whose significance has been elusive and which now, reified and repeated, seem to carry a conclusive signifying power. Yet still they evade our desire to make stable sense of them.

It's as if Handke's play forces us to experience the edge or grotesquery typical of the "modern" genre as if it were expressing a central fear about meaning and identity, about an anguish finally so private, so cut off from true communication, that it threatens to destroy the self. Flow seems to be purchased only at the price of submission to the accepted conventions of language and the subjections that follow from them. Hovering in the background, over the course of the play, there remains the longing for a different kind of flow that would be genuine and free. There are hints, flashes of unexpected poetry and wild hilarity, but they are painfully brief and apparently unsustainable. Language perpetuates our subjugation, and the characters find no lasting alternative to playing its empty power games, except by succumbing to a chaos of arbitrary identifications. Trying to free themselves, they fall through the ice. The climax makes any gesture of enlightenment, any escape from the nightmare, dubious if not derisory. Only by *playing* "waking up" can we continue to ride.

· VII ·

With an edge of anguish that feels surprisingly raw and unassimilated after almost thirty years, *The Ride across Lake Constance* addresses what might be called the *modern crisis of privacy*. This is an issue of central importance to both modern culture and modern drama and indeed to anything that may be presumed to come "after" the modern. It is no accident that the terrible puzzle over self and language, persons and texts, that constitutes the post-structuralist or postmodernist moment is coeval with what appear to be the final stages of this crisis of privacy. Our radical doubts about selfhood and identity seem the inevitable product of a long history of increasingly excruciating scrutiny of inward, private spaces.

When Elizabeth I rescued England from the horrors of religious persecution by requiring no more than an outward conformity from her subjects, she declared that she would not open a window into men's souls; it may be said that she left it to Shakespeare to do so. By positing the existence of a newly crucial space for personal decision, where the deepest forms of feeling, understanding, and self-direction were understood to intersect, the European era of religious struggle seems to have created the very privacy it sought sometimes to violate, sometimes to guard.

We have been staring into Elizabeth's window for more than four hundred years now, and gradually our gaze has become an X ray. The current snapshot of what is inside our heads is shadowy, disturbing, hard to relate to ordinary appearances. If a personal inner space remains even today the most precious and defining thing about us, the modern crisis of privacy springs from the fact that this space has become (1) infinitely permeable and manipulable from outside—a network of constructions, subjugations, genes, and ideologies, the helpless product of media, markets, and molecular biology; and (2) infinitely recessive, fragmented, and self-alienating from within—the thousand burdened meanings *Je est un autre* has taken on since Rimbaud.

It is not simply the swing of intellectual fashion from individualism to collectivism that accounts for the cloud that now hovers over the idea of the private self, nor is it the case that a newly powerful sense of history has in some way proved that the self is itself only an intellectual fashion. A host of modern phenomena have combined to create the crisis. To take only some of the most recent: Sophisticated electronic surveillance and the universal sharing of information make private life virtually unprotectable. Political life, especially in the United States, seems increasingly to be carried on by means of minute questioning of officials about personal matters. "The subpoenas issued by Starr and Klayman are perfectly legal under current law, but a hundred years ago many of them would have been suppressed as clear violations of privacy." Paradoxically, this legal development seems to have been prompted by a growing worry about *protecting* privacy. Erosion of the Fourth Amendment, as

Jeffrey Rosen has pointed out, is based on a fear of penetration, the idea that there exist schemes—such as those of organized crime, foreign agents, or terrorists—for secretly degrading us.

The more that we think we know about how selves are constructed, the more open to violation they appear. We are properly concerned over the fragility of personal development, especially in the vulnerable cases of children, women, the poor, racial minorities . . . but the list has become so long it is clear that we all feel vulnerable. We fear the power of drugs, pornography, hate speech, child molesters, the mob. Yet our fear of what can thwart or distort development has led to a call for curbs on many hard-won legal rights usually connected with privacy. And, while we struggle with these questions, the portrait of the self drawn by psychoanalysis, neurophysics, and philosophy grows increasingly complex, not to say chaotic. It is diffuse, decentered, overdetermined, abjected and subjected, perhaps simply illusory. Today the position of many intellectuals seems to be *there is no self and its rights must be protected.*

As a social matter—and ultimately even as an individual matter—the questions of privacy raised here are really questions of *intimacy*. For the realm of the private depends on our not being alone. It is through the presence and pressure of others that we discover what is ours. Privacy is other people. But, through intimacy with certain of these others, we define what is private by sharing—or withholding it. It is through intimacy that the private self reveals its uncertain, vulnerable outlines.

Intimacy is defined by privacy but also creates it. If intimacy is the coming together of two privacies, the private self may be said to discover itself through intimate contact.

Even the etymology of *intimacy* reflects this mutual relation with privacy. The roots of the word suggest the ever-troubled impulse of Western culture to colonize and imperialize the self. *Intimacy* comes from the Latin superlative *intimus,* "most inward," and the impulse, the desire, perhaps the need to achieve a superlative degree of inwardness, has haunted European thought since who-knows-when. Augustine charts the depths of his soul through contacts with mother, lover, teacher, friend. We call certain relationships intimate because, in them, *intimus* speaks to *intimus,* but *intimus* itself is discovered, nourished, invented, through intimacies—through love or its experimental extensions, reading, writing, art making.

When Elizabeth talks about the window, she is saying I don't have to get religiously intimate with my subjects; their privacy in this matter should be safe from the state—thereby raising the question, as we have seen, of just what that protected privacy might contain, what layers of inwardness a religious conscience might draw upon or reveal. All this is reflected by the tense passage in the history of the English language when a more specialized idea of consciousness begins to break away from the notion of "conscience." "Thus conscience doth make cowards of us all"; Claudius spies on Hamlet while he says this, but he lacks the skill, which Shakespeare reserves for the audience, to see through the window he's opened. Actually, Shakespeare in large part *creates* this skill in his audience, which is to say that he is one of the primary inventors of modern consciousness. It is the complex inwardness Shakespeare imagines for his hero that leads to the tortured intimacies of Hamlet's scene with his mother, an exchange without parallel in the history of drama to 1600. Four centuries later *Kika* is still on the case, probing the question of what sorts of intimacy different kinds of genre are comfortable with—a question so self-reflexive as to undermine our own intimacy with the work of art. Our peep through the window now catches us in the posture of voyeurs. The policing of bodily fluids and the ubiquity of movie cameras raise exemplary problems about filmmaking—and modern privacy.

Clearly, any attack on the coherence or integrity of the private self disturbs the terms of intimate contact. As privacy has grown problematic, fragmented, X ray–like, so intimacy has similarly been shadowed, thrown into doubt. With Freud the picture of adult relationships turns spectral; they are the reenactments of childhood experiences, the ghosts of our parents twining and beckoning. The problem with Freud's famous model of the sexual act is not that there are four people involved in it but that none of them is you.

Over the past century there has developed the disconcerting sense that the more you press to intimacy with someone else, the more you feel alone—alone with a privacy that feels at once bottomless and shallow,

inescapable and unreal. Freud's spectral evacuation of
the intimate haunts the modern discourse of intimacy—
whether as cause or symptom it is impossible to say.
While fictional representations of intimate contact have
become more and more detailed and explicit, not only
in sexual matters but in the increasingly nuanced por-
trayal of consciousness and speech, the exchanges
reported are increasingly unsatisfactory. Intimate scenes
are likely to be stumbling, aborted, painfully inept.

Certainly, from the point of view of drama the crisis
of privacy is best understood as a crisis of intimacy. Theater's concern with the private is always with the
moment when one inwardness meets another, the
onstage contact between two lives as well as our own
spying, as audience, on private and intimate moments. A
history of intimacy in drama would be worth writing.
What is most revealing for our purposes, however, is the
way the crisis of intimacy has been expressed in modern
drama.

Modern naturalistic acting depended from its begin-
nings on a kind of alienated intimacy. Dialogue in Ibsen
and Chekhov works by the interaction of submerged
currents of intention, more or less hidden from their
speakers, that run beneath the words spoken by the
characters—their subtexts, as we have learned to call
them. But the very notion of subtext, as its inventor
Stanislavsky uses it, reflects a pre-crisis mentality.
Superficially, at least, it suggests confidence in a locat-
able, coherent internal life, expressible as motivation,
though Stanislavsky himself introduced a potential

source of confusion from the start by calling this inner life "unconscious." In any case, the confidence was already out of date, already undermined by the great nineteenth-century dramatists, in whose plays motives are often multiple, irrational, contradictory, obscure. When Gregers and Hedvig or Astrov and Yelena have their intimate talks, the most powerful contact between them occurs outside the range of their conscious understanding.

Throughout modern drama the peculiar climaxes I spoke of earlier, where projects of enlightenment break off and gutter into absence, are usually marked by grim discoveries about intimacy. A murderous component reveals itself amid expressions of intense tenderness at the end of *Rosmersholm* and *The Iceman Cometh*. Three centuries after Hamlet's scene with Gertrude, how do an enlightened mother and son at last speak truthfully together? See *Ghosts*. In *The Balcony* the revolutionary hero's self-castration marks the failure of his project of true intimacy with Chantal. Enrico IV's play-long efforts to prove to his tormentors the superiority of his grasp of the construction of the self issue in a desperate attempt to embrace a frightened young woman dressed up like his unfaithful fiancée of twenty years ago.

Failed attempts at intimacy form a central trope in modern drama. Though privacy may depend on our not being alone, the terrible revelation of many twentieth-century treatments of intimacy is that we are in fact unappeasably isolated. The sense of absolute alienation amid scenes of intimate contact, deliberately exaggerated in *Ride,* is common. Enrico remembers staring into the face of his beloved:

> How awful it is to have to flounder, the way I have, in the thought of this terrible thing which drives one truly mad: that if you are next to someone and looking into her eyes—the way I looked one day into a certain person's eyes—then you can imagine what it is like to be a beggar in front of a door through which you shall never be able to enter.

Ride's account of such failures of intimacy as failures of flow, as a kind of "freezing," is anticipated in Brecht's early *In the Jungle of Cities,* a play that is shaped as an obsessive battle to achieve intimacy in the capitalist jungle:

> The generations stare coldly into each other's eyes. If you cram a ship's hold full of human bodies, so it almost bursts—there will be such loneliness in that ship that they'll all freeze to death.

Pinter, too, hits on a memorable image of frozen flow in one of the many grotesque versions of intimacy he delineates in his plays. Hirst, the alcoholic poet in *No Man's Land,* sees both flow and freezing as terrifying, alienating:

> When I stood my shadow fell upon her. She looked up. Give me the bottle . . . I hate drinking alone. There's too much solitary shittery.

What was it? Shadows. Brightness, through leaves
. . . In the bushes. Young lovers. A fall of water. It
was my dream . . . Who was drowning in my dream?

It was blinding. I remember it. I've forgotten. By
all that's sacred and holy. The sounds stopped. It was
freezing. There's a gap in me. I can't fill it. There's a
flood running through me. I can't plug it. They're
blotting me out.

While Brecht moves sharply away from the subject
after *Jungle,* Pinter has made the crisis of intimacy his
central theme. Pinter's characters typically combine
projects of making intimate contact with an hysterical
fear of contact. (Cf. Davies' fear in *The Caretaker* that gas
is escaping from a disconnected stove, that electricity
will attack him from an open socket; Aston spends the
play ineffectually trying to fix an electric plug.) They
defend themselves by a bewildering series of put-ons,
ventriloquisms, and role-playing games. In these games
the private self threatens to disappear into its linguistic
repertory.

For Pinter's characters contact with another person is
like entering Bolsover Street, the strange cul-de-sac that
the thuggish Briggs describes in *No Man's Land.* The
"intricate one-way" traffic system allows you to get in
but makes it impossible to get out. For everyone in this
play and in Pinter generally the object in human relations seems to be to get in, make contact, and get out
without being trapped, without being touched in turn.
The actor's entry in performing Pinter must be tuned to

the anxious ingenuity of such maneuvers, the expertness and parodic deftness of each feint, the running score of the game. The actor must also be responsive to what is absent—avoided, feared, frozen, unavailable—in the characters' language.

To the Arts and Leisure pages Pinter's *Mountain Language* seemed a new "political" departure. In fact, it is an unusually explicit statement of his underlying theme, with a crucial scene that revealingly links the problem of intimacy to questions about gender and language. The mother of a political prisoner is finally allowed to speak in her native tongue, long forbidden by the state, but after so many years she cannot. Barely concealed by the dialogue is a buried metaphor, "the mother tongue":

PRISONER: Mother, I'm speaking to you. You see? We can speak. You can speak to me in your own language.

She is still.

You can speak.

Pause.

Mother. Can you hear me? I am speaking to you in your own language.

Pause.

Do you hear me?

Pause.

It's our language.

Pause.

Can't you hear me? Do you hear me?

She does not respond.

Mother?

GUARD: Tell her she can speak in her own language.
New rules. Until further notice.
PRISONER: Mother?
She does not respond. She sits still.
The Prisoner'*s trembling grows. He falls from the chair on to his knees, begins to gasp and shake violently.*
The Sergeant *walks into the room and studies the* Prisoner *shaking on the floor.*
SERGEANT: (*To* Guard) Look at this. You go out of your way to give them a helping hand and they fuck it up.

It seems clear that the voice we regularly hear in Pinter is the language of the father, spoken by people denied access to the mother tongue.

Whether the mother tongue is ever spoken in Pinter and what, if spoken, it might sound like remain subjects for future investigation. My guess is that we hear it occasionally in the speech of some of his women and very rarely, with painful obliquity, in a few of his men. But what is important here is the remarkable, enabling tension that the search for a lost ground of intimacy can achieve on the contemporary stage. (It is this embattled, feminized ground of intimacy, I think, that Pinter refers to in the title of *No Man's Land*.) Whatever the lost language of the mother may be, Pinter has pursued it as circumspectly and done as much to invest it with reality as any recent seeker after an *écriture féminine*.

When it is written, the history of intimacy in drama will also surely note the new problems of performance that have been created by advanced twentieth-century attempts to deal with the crisis of intimacy. Not only in

Pirandello and Pinter but in writers like Beckett, Adrienne Kennedy, Caryl Churchill, and Sam Shepard, performance is forced to look beyond the solutions of Stanislavsky, Brecht, or Artaud. Projecting a self that is radically fragmented, occluded, self-fleeing, self-undermined, the modern actor must increasingly seek new relations with the text, new modes of entry.

From a theatrical point of view these problems are often more far-reaching than may at first appear. While Beckett's plays, for example, are frequently and successfully performed, we have as yet only a very uncertain grasp of the distinctive style of playing that they both require and make possible. Think of the questions of attack, of authenticity, that are raised by the following speech of Hamm's in *Endgame:*

> I once knew a madman who thought the end of the world had come. He was a painter—and engraver. I had a great fondness for him. I used to go and see him, in the asylum. I'd take him by the hand and drag him to the window. Look! There! All that rising corn! And there! Look! The sails of the herring fleet! All that loveliness! (*Pause.*) He'd snatch away his hand and go back into his corner. Appalled. All he had seen was ashes. (*Pause.*) He alone had been spared. (*Pause.*) Forgotten (*Pause.*) It appears the case is . . . was not so . . . so unusual.

This passage figures a very complex theatrical moment. Hamm is playing a part, the rather unlikely one of a younger Hamm imagined as an exponent of the beauties of nature. He speaks of a world outside a recollected window, toward which he gestures, performing the role of his younger self. But, in the world that the theater audience sees, he is waving toward a wall beyond which all is "corpsed." Or, rather, toward a world reported by Clov and believed by Hamm to be so. Hamm's pauses, his uncertainty, allow multiple possibilities of delusion or recognition to be felt. Was the painter mad, or did he see more deeply than Hamm? Is Hamm's current conviction that the world outside is ashes any more verifiable than his mad friend's? And what does *our* world really look like—is it Disneyland or Hiroshima? Our possible positions, either as affirming or denying that the world we live in is as dead, barren, and meaningless as Hamm and *Endgame* represent it to be, are undermined evenhandedly.

What kind of performance is adequate to such radical doubt? What source of truth in acting does it imply? Like Hamm himself, the actor playing Hamm waves at the walls of a stage beyond which nothing can be verified. The speech about the madman is marked by the continuous and convincing rhythms of naturalistic reminiscence, yet how is the actor supposed to relate them to the rest of his performance, which clearly requires other styles than naturalism? Where is the link between the speech just quoted and lines like:

HAMM: Can there be misery (*he yawns*) loftier than
    mine? No doubt.

And how, even in the speech itself, are Hamm's large, inevitably ironic gestures, Pozzo-like in their inflation (the herring fleet! the rising corn!) to be located? How does the actor achieve the kind of calling into question that lines like these require and still stay true to the poignant naturalistic rhythms in which they are embedded? What in the role allows these naturalistic rhythms to arise?

For an actor or director the effect requires closer examination than can be given here, but what is involved may be described as a combination of subtexts, roughly identifiable as Stanislavskian, Brechtian, Artaudian, Pirandellian, and even Shavian. All are abundantly present in *Waiting for Godot, Endgame,* and *Happy Days.* The crucial point about them is that in performance no subtext may be given priority over any other. To use an overworked critical term, which in this case seems apposite: no subtext may be treated as privileged.

This is in sharp contrast to the standard convention of modern subtexts before Beckett, in which the subtext is understood to represent the authentic source of the text. The character may not be in touch with the source, but the actor is. In the Stanislavskian system the character may not be aware of the drives or inhibitions that run beneath the text of a Hedda or a Lopakhin, but the actor makes them available to the audience as a truth in terms of which the text can be understood. In the Brechtian system this privileged truth lies in the actor's commitment to the social interpretation of the character, which give the *gestus* its effect. But it would contradict Beckett's vision to offer such a possibility of authentication. Thus, our engagement with the actors, though it can be intense, must not be confidently located. We must not be allowed to feel, "Yes, I can get behind these appearances." It is clear, for example, that Beckett rejects any performance mode that invites the audience in. The preference is for Keaton's style over Chaplin's—there can be no cozy sharing of a human essence. In the same way there can be no privileging of the music-hall routine over the Artaudian anguish or vice versa. This refusal of any privileged structuring of subtexts is the absolute condition of authenticity in Beckett performance.

When Didi and Gogo go through their vaudeville/circus/music-hall routines, one can also hear the Artaudian subtext of anguished acknowledgment of the void, of what Pozzo calls "talking in a vacuum." But the anguish, for all its intensity, does not achieve priority over the routine and make it merely a vehicle or veil for the anguish. We have no way of saying that the anguish isn't a routine too. Any actor who wants to insist that he is "more than" a clown at this point will be denying the truth of his anguish. To move truthfully among the varied textualities demanded of the Beckett actor is to make a very delicate assertion of individual presence, whose authenticating attack must never slop over into a spurious claim for authenticity. It requires an acting that seeks to become *insignificant enough.*

There is a kind of egalitarianism in Beckett, easily overlooked, though it helps explain the concreteness, the kind of earthy intimacy Beckett actors can achieve in performance. Given the lack of any ground for action, given the terrifying silence of the infinite spaces, action, though in one sense impossible in Beckett, is in another sense everywhere and in anything; it simply goes with being human. The most trivial activities—taking off a shoe, letting an alarm clock ring to the end, reading the small print on a toothbrush—are as significant as the greatest undertakings because, for Beckett, every attempt at action is a metaphysical encounter between human restlessness and the fact that there is nothing to be done. Any kind of activity confronts the ground of our being, although habit is a great deadener, and ordinarily we do not recognize that the encounter is taking place.

Again, meaning is everywhere because we are here and can't avoid being here. We are stuck in being, a circumstance that becomes terrifyingly literal in *Happy Days*. Because we are stuck in being, we have nothing to do but play against the great negation that apparently encompasses us. And so Winnie, for example, grips us like a heroine, and we are uncomfortable with this sensation and think there must be something more heroic, more significant (or "really insignificant"), than filing your nails and claiming it's a wonderful day. But from Beckett's point of view *that's* the sentimental proposition. Winnie grips us, as the other great Beckett characters grip us, a center of action amid all the disauthenticating texts that she must play. I think that as critics we become easily muddled about these very ordinary heroes, exceptional only in the extremity of their ordinariness, their immobility, self-deception, and restlessness. Like us, they are citizens of the great democracy of the scandal of human existence.

Perhaps surprisingly, the idea of nonprivileged subtexts turns out to be helpful in understanding not only Beckett but many more recent and more obviously political performance texts. In particular, it may sharpen our appreciation of innovative works that have an interest in problems of identity, especially when they deal with the struggles of marginalized or oppressed groups. Some sort of help is needed here, because a lot of criticism intended to support such works seems to fail to appreciate what's best about them. Politically committed discussion seems to run into difficulty in sorting out theatrical responses that engage the modern problematic of privacy. It tends to miss the complex portrait and performance of identity that such works can offer, in favor of certain simplifications. At bottom these amount to insisting that only certain subtexts may be treated as valid. The source of this critical difficulty is the problem of matching the political urgency of great projects of emancipation to the troubling X rays of modern privacy, to understandings of the self that call into question individual, to say nothing of collective, identity.

Feminist performance, for example, is notably concerned with the multiple texts and entrances, the intricate play of identifications, that obstruct or empower female identity. And feminist performance theory has certainly been alert to these theatrical possibilities. Still there's a tendency, even in such theatrically sensitive work as Elin Diamond's recent, important *Unmaking Mimesis,* to view feminist performance basically as discursive, a stable, privileged subtextual commentary on social roles, history, and politics.

Diamond has written with great insight about the interweaving of identifications in playwrights like Adrienne Kennedy and Caryl Churchill. She has a keen sense of the complexity of the plays she is examining, but certain simplifications creep in. It is possible that she has limited her analysis by accepting too readily the narrow view of identification that Brecht puts forward in his theoretical writings. There, as Diamond notes, he portrays theatrical identification as *einfühlung,* empathy, the naturalistic abolition of distance. This may explain her readiness to read alternative forms of performance as a type of demonstration, in which an actor points, as with a ruler, at a character and its place in the ensemble of social relations.

I don't mean to undervalue Diamond's own theoretical contribution or the balance she strives to maintain. She makes it emphatically clear that she wants to preserve the idea of the audience's emotional involvement with character as somehow valid in spite of Brecht, just as she wants to feminize mimesis by freeing it from a presumed subservience to a male-defined reality. Her objections to the fetishizing gaze and to the cultural prejudices that underlie much naturalistic theater are valid enough, but her search for ways to break out of the closed circuit of patriarchal ideology leads her finally to see the play of identifications in the theater as a series of readable (or deliberately occluded) signs in what is, though quite sophisticated, at bottom a Brechtian scheme (she calls her method "gestic criticism").

Brecht's *practice,* of course, is far more complex than this, and so, happily, is Diamond's. Still, one remains concerned that feminist performance theory, especially when it lacks Diamond's subtlety, runs the risk of not fully connecting with the theatrical imagination. This is the price of insisting, as so often seems to be the case, on the privileging of certain positions from which to construe identity, especially the position of the spectator presumed to know. (What this spectator knows is usually Marx, but it is the presumption of knowledge, rather than the specific politics, that is the problem.)

For the audience of any art, response always begins with some Coleridgean I-am, some movement of entry answering to the imaginative possibilities of the work before it. In the case of drama this movement is multiplied by the active creative presence of actors. In this heady mix of identifications and bodies it is a dangerous academic reflex to privilege the "reading" of a distanced, ironic A+ spectator/professor. We don't read Shakespeare to show off for the class but to enlarge our lives.

Even with such an ostensibly cool and Brechtian performer as the great Anna Deveare Smith, I don't find that my response is to anything like a demonstration, a classroom comparison of subject positions. I "learn" by becoming intimate with the immense range of Smith's modes of entering a text that she has created out of the words of her own real-life characters, a range that encompasses mimicry, empathy, selection and narration, and passional as well as ironic commentary. Nor does Smith encourage me to privilege one of these modes over the others and to interpret them in its light. When the performance is over, I have enlarged my repertory of psychic movement, have shared in a mixture (to describe it in crude shorthand) of tenderness, objectivity, and appetite for life, a mixture that reflects the power of Smith's unique contribution to modern performance style, perhaps the most important since Grotowski.

It is only fair to add that Diamond's impulse as a critic seems often toward an appreciation of the processual, hors-textual, bodily aspect of theater and indeed intermittently toward a kind of deprivileging. She is aware of the complicated bodily life of the plays she is examining and eager to make that life count for something in analysis. But, more often than not, the sense of theater as a demonstration prevails. Admittedly, it's a difficult balance for a politically committed criticism to strike. I wonder, though, whether the conception of acting I've been trying to develop here might not make it easier to avoid the privileging that seems inevitably to come with a tendency to treat subtext simply as another form of text, spectatorship simply as a reading of signs, and perhaps simply with the urgencies of any political agenda.

This is not the place to explore at length the complex political questions that are raised by our troubled late-modern notions of privacy and intimacy, selfhood and performance. One point may be worth noting, however. Ultimately, the radical engagement of twentieth-century drama with the crisis of intimacy seems to return us—as in Beckett's egalitarianism or Smith's breadth and balance of identification—to some version of the well-worn democratic issue of respect for the individual. Respect for the individual! Hardly are these words out than the crisis itself seems to slouch a bit more clearly into view. To contemplate the odd vibrations that rise from the page when this phrase appears is to feel very strongly the curious contemporary status of self-hood and privacy. "Respect for the individual"—this would seem immediately identifiable as a fatuous phrase in a fatuous bourgeois mouth, but at the same time it's what you and I would want to teach our children and compel our legislators to honor. The paradox is part of the crisis, and, as with everything that has to do with drama, it's as much public as private. Politically, it's all a matter of taking the ride across Lake Constance. The idea of the individual self, with its meaningful, valuable inwardness, may be too fragile to support our weight—but we must trust our journey to it. In such writers as Habermas and even the later Wittgenstein we find hints as to what, ethically, it might mean to take this ride.

Here, however, it is necessary to stress only that the ride *is* a paradox and that the paradox cannot be evaded—though at different historical moments it may take different cultural forms, pressing now one, now another, aspect of our experience toward crisis. In the Gospels the great moment of satire occurs when a politi-

cian uses a fashionable deconstructive phrase to evade
ethical commitment. Today jesting Pilate would say, not
What is truth? but *What is the self?* The point of the para-
ble, however, remains the same. One must stay for an
answer. Unsatisfactory or absurd as it may be, to be
stuck in being is to be compelled to make meanings.
Simply in order to live, we cannot help acting like actors
who enter a text—as if from a self, as if to posit a share-
able/unshareable *intimus,* a privacy, an identity. Today
our understanding of that *intimus* has become so complex
that it is tempting to try to do away with it altogether, to
insist that the self has no substance, no depth, no core of
agency, to say there is no self, nothing outside the text,
nothing but texts—verbal, social, economic, mathemat-
ical, neurological texts out of which the illusion for-
merly known as the self is constructed. Thus we reduce
the self simply to one text among others. It is possible to
take this view, of course, but impossible to deny that
finally even this view comes into being only through the
act of someone who takes it. The private self may not
exist, but it must act; no meaning appears without it.
The actor must enter a text; there is no other way to be
an actor. Nor is there any other way for a text to *be.*
Whenever a text speaks, a self has spoken.

Our new difficulties about intimacy and identity raise new questions about recognition—dramatic and otherwise. What kind of acknowledgment or discovery is to be expected when one dissolving, inaccessible, possibly nonexistent self confronts another? Once again, *The Ride across Lake Constance* helps us approach the problem. We have seen that in its treatment of flow and intimacy *The Ride across Lake Constance* takes up and exaggerates theatrical motifs that are crucially familiar to twentieth-century audiences—it is a play to end all plays but especially modern ones. More radically than anything in Ionesco, it directs us to a madness at the base of language that explodes the very foundations of identity. It is interesting, then, that at its climax flow is restored and freezing overcome, if only momentarily, by a kind of primitive prelinguistic recognition, a child confronted by a face:

> *The* Woman *holds it in such a way that the* Child *sees* Bergner *from the front. It stops bawling at once.*

This is richly suggestive, especially in the context of the play's shattering critique of language and selfhood. The moment draws its force from much that is formative in human development; it speaks to both the shaping of identity and the capacity for intimate exchange.

It will be recalled that there are actually two moments of face-to-face "recognition" in this final sequence. The second comes at the very end:

> Von Stroheim *gets up and bends down to her . . . She opens her eyes and recognizes* Von Stroheim; *she begins to smile.*

What Bergner recognizes when she sees Von Stroheim is radically uncertain. Whether she is continuing to "play," and whether this play is liberating or enslaving, whether we are in fact returning to the degrading power games in which Von Stroheim has involved her—these are questions that *Ride*'s final darkness does nothing to resolve. Still, the smile, the awakening, the recapitulation of motifs, the focus on the figure who has "gone through" the most in the play, even the contrast with darkness, all deliberately remind us of the classical role that recognition plays in drama. This links it, too, even more closely with Bergner's earlier irenic moment with the child.

Here Handke is obviously referring to the very radical of recognition, the ur-recognition of parent and child. It is out of an infant's encounter with its mother's face that the earliest and most crucial passages of self-construction are negotiated. As we have seen, these moments involve constant change on the part of both child and mother; they are fraught with varying presentations and identifications.

Clearly, the scanning and interpreting of a mother's face is a process repeated and refigured in thousands of adult encounters. Faces are above all what we recognize, the most obvious examples of an object of recognition. It would not be too much to say that all recognitions, not only dramatic ones, echo the original encounter between mother and child. In a face, a looming portent rich with mood, detail, intention, nuance, expectation, the child discovers a notion of self and world, from which the idea of meaning itself only emerges later. It is an earlier, more expansive and enabling passage than Lacan's mirror stage (to say nothing of being more clinically grounded). Surely it is in a presiding, answering face rather than in a mirror that we first read self and its profile and what sustains the self. Indeed, it may be in scanning a face that we first discover what "reading" is. And the anxious tension, the relief, the comic and tragic registrations that collect around recognition in drama, are all present in the infant's responses to its mother's face.

A face is our first great source of stimulus toward the world, rousing, supporting, troubling, our expectations. But, if this face has the power to still our crying, make us smile, foster and set in play our sense of self *as* self, it can also be a source of apprehension and self-collapse. Through a well-known experiment called the "still-face procedure," psychologists have carefully charted the perturbations that occur whenever a mother's face becomes unresponsive. Simply by ceasing to change expression, a mother's face can powerfully disturb her baby. The withdrawal of agency, of reference-towards, promotes an ontological crisis, a sentiment of radical betrayal. What is lost is not merely a supportive outside presence but an inner coherence, a confidence in the very existence of the self. There is no there there; the saving essence has vanished.

So the mother's face both presides over and has the power to destroy our earliest loomings of meaning and identity. For the rest of our life we will seek to read our fate in others' faces. We search them for our happiness and value. We insist on trying, as Shakespeare's Duncan sadly warns us we cannot, to find the mind's construction there. We read deep understanding of the self in Rembrandt's portraits; they persuade us that truly to see a face is to have access to a soul.

By the same token, the modern crisis of intimacy can be read in modern art's uneasiness about the face. It's not that we no longer have important renderings of faces, but the face seems to present a special problem among the new modalities of the visible. There is an uncertainty about its rendering, like the gestures of someone not sure what to do with his hands. This is not merely another example of the crisis of representation, though it suggests that a crisis of *self*-representation may underlie our general philosophical doubts about reference and signification. The "straight" portrait somehow becomes unavailable; it feels banal, derivative. The face vanishes or recedes or becomes a mask or a pair of eyes or a flat sign, a couple of crudités curled on a cheeseboard; it reappears screaming or flayed, eaten from within or by the painter's stare.

The face in twentieth-century art reflects a contradictory response, nowhere more apparent than in the work of Picasso, who typically offers us two very different kinds of faces, both on view nearly throughout his career. The first is radically antihumanist—the face as an armature on which certain organs may be wound, an alien array of forms. This face is an object, a body part. Its eyes may do the work of seeing, but they don't see *us;* there's no one at home peeping through these appearances. The second face, by contrast, is exquisite, inviting; it summons the familiar visage of the beloved with a few delicately modulated lines, a lyrical, tender graph of desire. Of all Picasso's styles this is the one that stands most apart from the rest of his work. It's as if the artist were saying, I must see you (my sleeping mistress, my child) this way in order not to see you *that* way.

Can any vision of a face awaken us, as at the end of *Ride,* from the crisis of intimacy, the death of the self, the prison house of language? Here one must turn to a philosophical response to the postmodern problematic of the self that is based on a discussion of the face—more specifically, on the idea of face-to-face encounter. For Emmanuel Lévinas the face is above all the sign of a primitive responsibility to the Other. Confronted with the absolute alterity of another face, I must respond; and only in responding do I have my being. Being is thus a product of the *en face* relation, rather than the reverse. "Preexisting the plane of ontology is the ethical plane." Even if one is not prepared to assign to ethics such originary status, Lévinas's account has the important effect of grounding language in the action of something outside language, in the response of one unique human individual, one world of infinite possibility, to another. Language is what is called forth by the separate, unassimilable, infinite possibility of the Other's face.

Lévinas also touches the argument of this book at another point, the connection we have been exploring between identity formation and dramatic acting, when acting is conceived as entry into a text. The links already suggested between acting, textuality, and identification are reinforced by Lévinas's view of the *en face* relation as one of substitution. As one commentator puts it, it involves literally putting oneself in another's place. And it is from this displacement, this journey beyond the self, that one's selfhood springs. I institute my subjectivity by subjecting myself to the otherness of the Other. I can't be me without you being other. I *am* my response—not only to my mother's changing face and to the other *philia* that have identified me in my deep past but to every face I encounter. My own face, my selfhood, can only be said to exist in its expressions of itself, and these expressions are grounded in the obligation to speak that other faces continually impose.

The originality of the face precedes language, which depends on it for communication. The relation of the unique face to the meanings it draws forth from the signifying systems of language corresponds exactly to the relation we have been developing between entry and text. Without the vectored uniqueness of the individual who speaks it—one face compelled by another face into the absolute instability of dialogue—without this prior movement, the text would remain literally meaningless, lost in the infinitely proliferating possibilities of signification:

> Language . . . presupposes the originality of the face without which, reduced to an action among actions whose meaning would require an infinite psychoanalysis or sociology, it could not commence.

By the same token, the constructions of language cannot exhaust the infinite human possibility of the individual speakers who give language meaning. Lévinas entitles one of his most important books *Totality and Infinity;* the "infinity" implied by each human face exceeds the "totality" of theories and other generalizing discourses. No comprehensive statement, no totalizing text, can be found that by itself will contain the truth of the *en face* dialogue, of which any human utterance is part:

> The [full face] conjuncture of the same and the other . . . is irreducible to totality.

This is the ethical side of the epistemological fact that the entry of an actor into a text cannot be reduced to a text.

All these visions, from Handke, Lévinas, and recent developmental psychology, of a face presiding over the emergent self in the process of self-identification—an enabling, fostering, interrupting, challenging face, opening the doors to dialogue, reference, meaning—have profound implications for the study of drama.

Genre itself, one might say, is the face of the dramatic enterprise hovering over the individual play. It is a face whose expression anticipates, amplifies, and feeds back to us the whole bodily engagement of performers, text, and audience. The face of the enterprise, as of the individual performers bent with full focused attention on what they are doing as they enter into the script. The face that soothes, the face that absorbs the howl. The face that recognizes, that is recognized and misrecognized and recognized again. The face as the very theater of recognition and identification, of self and other, the face that makes good the myth of the individual that grounds our humanness. It is a face that makes and redirects flow. (One could compare Yeats's "moon of comic tradition" at the end of *The Herne's Egg*. The same effect occurs with more complex force in *The Seagull* and *Waiting for Godot,* where again moon rise broadly hints that we are going to get more than we may have generically bargained for yet with a gesture that looks *almost* as if it's sealing a generic bargain.)

Not an inappropriate metaphor, the face, when we remember that comedy and tragedy are traditionally represented as faces, ostensibly separate but always linked, usually hovering before a curtain or over a stage. No, not as faces but as masks, those uncanny fusions of presence and absence, the human and the inanimate, death and life, made all the more haunting by the rigidity in their apparent emotion, asking to be filled with life. Genre: a vessel not quite closed at either end, into which the life of the performance flows and spreads.

So again we find in genre an aspect of drama that leads to an understanding of the way drama speaks to our lives. Genre as moonlike, overflowing, a presiding face—and, as such, a huge emblem, not only of how the dramatic text may glow with a suggestion of what awaits us when we enter a play, but an emblem of the textual aspect of life, which always asks us for more-than-text, and which appears already to bear upon itself an inviting or troubling answer to our entry; the changing face of the living text into which we each must enter in order to live, enter with the purposeful, playful, consuming *as if* of actors and audiences—as if we had a life, as if we were selves, as if we were we.

· IX ·

We are now in position to go back to Shakespeare and follow him in a notable investigation of flow at the boundaries of genre. *The Winter's Tale* is a play that elaborates in arresting fashion on the power of theatrical performance to tap into fundamental boundary crossings in human experience. Moreover, it connects these crossings with presiding, inviting, responsive female figures, whose expressions we are encouraged to think of as both rapidly changing and ultimately reassuring.

At the end of his career Shakespeare composes two odes to his dramatic company, *The Winter's Tale* and *The Tempest*. *Winter's Tale* invites us to share in the variety and superabundance of theater art in its fullest range of effects, especially as that art is exemplified by Shakespeare's great repertory ensemble, The King's Men, who can do everything from acrobatics to tragedy. One function of generic signs in *Winter's Tale* is to emphasize the heterogeneity of its theatrical materials. We are getting, the play regularly reminds us, *everything* this great creating company is capable of—an effect that is likely to overwhelm the pedantic classifying impulse, which can only exclaim, "Tragical-comical-pastoral!" in Polonius- or Ben Jonson–like amazement.

The boundary crossing from tragedy to comico-pastoral, from the wintry world of Sicily to Bohemia and spring, is emphasized by the play's famous bear, however one stages it.

> ANTIGONUS: Blossom, speed thee well!
> [*He lays down the* Baby.]
> There lie . . . A savage clamor!
> Well may I get aboard! This is the chase;
> I am gone forever. *Exit, pursued by a bear.*

As in *Kika,* the style gets funnier while the content gets grislier. In no other play is there a more brutal *sparagmos*—no other Shakespearean character is torn apart by a wild animal. Significantly, the transition is both sharp and blurry at the same time. Tragic and comic markers swirl together for much of the scene. The stage direction itself sounds comic, though a bear is one of Shakespeare's favorite tragic emblems. And the characters who enter as the bear chases poor Antigonus off the stage are a familiar pair of rustic clowns; their dialogue is replete with shtick even as it includes grotesque evocations of Antigonus' dismemberment.

Though this transition would seem to be decisive, it is in fact repeated several times in the course of acts 3 and 4. After apparently having crossed the boundary we find we are crossing it yet again, *always in the same direction.* Each transit involves striking generic alterations. At least three Astringers appear—the Bear, Time, and Autolycus; each marks a distinct break in dramatic style. And in each case the moments following the apparent break look back as well as forward, so that "Sicilian" images and generic hints reemerge just as we feel anew the onset of "Bohemian" expectations.

Not long after the final transition to the comical-pastoral world we get a remarkable speech in praise of the child that we saw abandoned in the bear scene, a child who in a few pages has suddenly grown up into a beautiful young woman—Sidney's very example of theatrical impropriety. This is Perdita, the queen of the feast, the presiding farmgirl/goddess of the sheep-shearing scene.

Perdita is one of Shakespeare's great parts, and, through her, *Winter's Tale* pursues its celebration of the ethical and psychological powers of performance. The seasonal and floral motifs in Perdita's dialogue with her lover, Prince Florizel, echo back to moments in the Sicilian tragedy of the first three acts and thereby gain a poignancy, a surprising sense of fullness in their present "comic" elaboration. Through Perdita the play funnels its vast range of sophistication into the sun-filled pleasures of a rural holiday feast. The character's reality for us—the part's remarkable performability—depends in this scene on Perdita's being simultaneously more and less of an "actress" than she thinks. Fiercely disliking artifice, Perdita, to her embarrassment, is dressed up (as a goddess) in a way that in fact more accurately expresses who she is (a divinely favored royal) than the identity (simple shepherdess) she believes is hers. She is the obedient daughter and innocent betrothed who effortlessly adds the roles of mother, queen of the feast, and passionate lover to her repertory of identifications. In spite of her shyness, she presides. She is the most elaborately responsive of hostesses in a play that is deeply concerned with hospitality, literally from beginning to end. Hospitality in *Winter's Tale* is linked to women's power to do the impossible, to connect tragically separated realms of experience—from Hermione's efforts to restore the playful bonds of childhood to two jealous adult males and to sustain royal graciousness at her sullen husband's court, to Paulina's little play-ending surprise for her guests—the return of Hermione from the dead. It is one of the many ways the play figures what is perhaps Shakespeare's most persistent theme: kindness, the secular power of individuals to better the human condition by acts of tenderness, mercy, solace, generosity.

The richness and fullness, the role-playing plangency of Perdita in this scene is associated with the theater but with theater in its closest proximity to the great occasions of ordinary life; the fullness comes from the sense of boundaries that ordinarily frame performance being crossed. It links the extraordinary qualities of the accomplished performer to the overwhelming fate-defying sweetness we can find in the simplest gestures of those we love. As such, it looks forward to the genre-bending miracles of the play's concluding scene, in which the dead Hermione's statue comes to life.

It is Florizel who praises Perdita, and his speech is of special interest to us because it is about flow:

> What you do
> Still betters what is done. When you speak, sweet,

I'd have you do it ever; when you sing,
I'd have you buy and sell so; so give alms,
Pray so; and for the ord'ring your affairs,
To sing them too. When you dance, I wish you
A wave o'th' sea, that you might ever do
Nothing but that—move still, still so,
And own no other function. Each your doing,
So singular in each particular,
Crowns what you are doing in the present deeds,
That all your acts are queens.

Florizel's speech celebrates what we would normally call Perdita's unaffected naturalness—but it also celebrates her grace of self-presentation. A presentation all the more theatrical because she is dressed up, pranked out like a goddess, "Flora peering in April's front." The speech, in fact, is also a description of a significant aspect of acting as an art. We like to watch a great actress or actor opening a letter or saying hello, because she does it so well. Not artificially, not affectedly, but (we want to say)—that's the way of it; we could watch her forever. Whatever Perdita does—whether she speaks or sings or dances—Florizel wishes she would simply go on doing it and never stop. In the context of *The Winter's Tale* the speech reminds us that in the gestures of a beautiful young person, as of an accomplished performer, we can feel in touch with the renewing energies of biological nature as well as with whatever we might mean by "grace," a word that is made to vibrate over its full range of secular and religious meanings in the course of the play.

We can better understand Florizel's description of Perdita if we think of Bernard Beckerman's useful distinction between performance and presentation. (Presentation is the character's represented behavior; performance is the way the actor represents it to us.) Perdita's performance always improves upon what she *presents* in performance. When Florizel wishes that Perdita would always dance and own no other function, he is wishing that she could be, as it were, "signifiering" (as opposed to signifying) forever:

> Each your doing
> So singular in each particular,
> Crowns what you are doing in the present deeds
> That all your acts are queens.

"What you are doing" may be compared to a text, a script for enactment, the kind of event or behavior we can abstract or decode from the moment (she is entertaining her father's guests, handing out flowers, smiling, etc.), while "each her doing" refers to her own entry as performer into the text of what she's doing (*Perdita* entertaining guests, Helen Mirren playing Perdita)—her singular way of doing what she does. And the sovereign result is the performance itself, considered as beyond textual boundaries—it is text expanded by other-than-text, script by acting, writing by life.

Similarly, in the statue scene, where the dead Queen returns to life, we are frequently reminded how

Hermione's human doings—breathing, body temperature, wrinkles—"crown" the statue that walks. The scene builds to its climax through exchanges that treat the mere reality of a middle-aged Hermione as if she were the greatest possible work of art. But the scene also builds on the paradoxical reality of acting. For any actor's performance to be convincing, we must feel the actor's entry as both alienating and involving, spontaneous and artful. We must both feel the entry and forget about it, accept the impossible movement to the Other, the return from the dead, all in a moment of flow. This basic aspect of acting is particularly tested by this kind of scene, whose "surprising" revelation we see coming well in advance (we see the text, as it were, long before the performance) and which we resist/desire because we think it can't possibly be made convincing. When the statue scene works in performance, as the testimony of actors and audiences attests, we move from understanding, abstractly, conceptually, that, yes, the statue is Hermione, we knew it all along, to *feeling* it with uncanny intensity—perhaps most often at Leontes's overwhelming and, quite literally, touching line, "Oh, she's warm!"

As this incredibly daring scene concludes, Shakespeare gives Paulina a wry comment that connects the play's tribute to performance with its provocative treatment of genre. It catches the primacy, the impact, of what performers achieve, of what the reunited couple achieves, in going beyond presentation, in bettering what is done. *What* they do is, after all—simply as what-is-done, simply as text—merely the argument of a typically unpersuasive old tale:

> That she is living
> Were it but *told* you, should be hooted at
> Like an old tale; but it appears she lives.

It does *appear* so indeed. Performance does more than simply transmit a text or tell a tale. Shakespeare is celebrating the fact that drama, this art of appearances, especially as his company can practice it, gets away with things, crosses boundaries that mere writing cannot.

Let us return for a moment to the rather different boundary crossings of *Ohio Impromptu*. A woman's face presides here too and leads us as in *Winter's Tale* to a moment of uncanny theatrical exaltation, but, instead of tapping into theater's deep connections with human kindness, with life's transforming moments of union and reunion, *Ohio Impromptu* draws on our equally radical intuitions of absence and isolation. In the end it dissolves what is apparently intimate into what may be no more than the illusions projected by an unbridgeable privacy.

If, as Nietzsche implies, all dramatic recognitions are a return from the dead, they can easily be made to express a burden of the most painful loneliness. Such loneliness haunts the final moments of *Ohio Impromptu* when the "sad tale" ceases and the identically dressed and bearded Reader and Listener look in each other's faces for the first and last time with an unfathomable recognition, "Unblinking. Expressionless." Remarkably, Nietzsche elsewhere offers what amounts to a penetrating insight into *Ohio Impromptu*'s treatment of human separation and isolation. It comes in a passage in which he describes the pain of communicating with a dead lover in terms that seem so closely to echo the circumstances of Beckett's play that they may well be a source for it:

With thee, beloved voice, with thee, the last remembered breath of all human happiness, let me discourse, even if it is only for another hour. Because of thee, I delude myself as to my solitude and lie my way back to multiplicity and love, for my heart shies away from believing love is dead. It cannot bear the icy shivers of loneliest solitude. It compels me to speak as though I were two . . . No one converses with me beside myself, and my voice reaches me as the voice of one dying.

In the *Ohio Impromptu* a "dear face" seems to preside. She has sent the Reader to the Listener to recite the Listener's own story—or so the story seems to tell us. But finally the beloved face is available, as in Nietzsche's account, only as a voice, produced from a text of unknown origin by a Reader who is a double double, uncannily resembling both the Listener and the figure described in the narrative, who mourns the loss of the beloved face and who listens to a reader tell this story. The mutually constitutive relation of text and performance is emphasized here as in few plays, but its impact is to dissolve the beloved face even more painfully in a series of receding perspectives. Has the narrator produced the text or the text the narrator? Is the play inside the story or the story inside the play? Does the "dear face" refer to a real person, or is it merely an effect of the text? My loneliness can be comforted only by a series of meditations that ultimately confirm that loneliness, self-performed fictions that are poignantly indistinguishable from my isolation and my sense of loss. My self-describing self may be the only face I see.

Deluding myself in my solitude, recalling—or imagining—"multiplicity and love," I am compelled, as Nietzsche puts it, "to speak as though I were two." To dramatize this fact, as in *Ohio Impromptu,* is to make active what is most deeply potent in drama—the way its pleasures sharpen our awareness of all the metaphysical impossibilities/necessities on which human restlessness is founded—that one can become another, that one can become oneself, that action is possible, that identification can be free, that identity can be both stable and open. What is expressed is nothing less than the heartbreaking promise of consciousness to redeem being, to console us with intimations of *intimus* and intimacy, to render life complete.

Whom do we applaud at the end of *Ohio Impromptu?* At the end of *Waiting for Godot* we applaud as we applaud at a play of Shakespeare's or Ibsen's. We applaud the actors for their activity, their journey, their skill in the contest, stimulated by the identifications they have elicited. But the twin longbeards of *Ohio Impromptu* remain more recessed from us, perhaps more recessed *in* us. They have been almost immobile, restricted—doubled not as in the tennis doubles athleticism of *Comedy of Errors,* say, but in a way that stresses their function as parts of a strangely haunting pattern. Perhaps we applaud the effectiveness of the pattern, the careful preparation of that persistent, vibrating final image that we may find expanding in our minds in the moment of darkness after the play is over, stretching the boundaries of perception, creating a "deep of the mind." But in the end the star of the piece is the beloved face, which we can never see because it is our own.

The exchange between inside and outside so intensely foregrounded by drama may finally remind us of what is most poignant in that exchange, our awareness of an element irremediably private in our experience. Theatrical framing devices, of which genre is one, provide a field in which intrapersonal events—private events that we recognize as ours by their insistent overwhelming of internal boundaries, as for example through tears and laughter—in which intrapersonal events can become transpersonally recognizable. They become transpersonal in the coming together of the multiple communal fields of theater—in which we are aware of ourselves as part of an audience, in the presence of actors, entering into scripts, "we" and "they" responding to identifications, joining together in a mutual act of becoming other.

The idea of genre as a face is actually an idea about how theater supports such mutualities, makes them possible and satisfying even when they are painful. It is an idea about theater that we have reached by way of genre, rather than simply an idea about genre. As such, it includes such notions as genre, mood, atmosphere, expectation, all the things that contribute to the tonality of our theatrical interest, experienced as in some way reassuring, supportive of flow. The reassurance can take the form of disturbance, of course; the face's expression may change, grow rigid or inscrutable, withdraw, be broken off. Indeed, the anxiety and stimulation of these breaks can never be entirely absent from the theatrical moment. Thus, modern theater's grim adequacy to the crisis of privacy.

As in *Ohio Impromptu* and the anguished undertext of *Ride across Lake Constance,* the pain of the inescapably private, the fact of irremediable loss, remains a central part of the dramatic equation—as is plain in even so comforting a piece as *The Winter's Tale.* Perdita's flow in the face of loss does not alter the fact that her brother is dead, that the bear long ago dined on Antigonus, that Hermione and Leontes have lost sixteen years and grown old. It's not that in the theater, or any art, the private becomes communal but that a movement from one to the other can take place, a kind of negotiation, a brushing together of identifications, with benefit to both. Intimacy and *intimus* expand without coinciding. We "shake hands," in the words of *The Winter's Tale,* "as over a vast." Like many more famous lines in the last plays, this may be one of Shakespeare's final thoughts on the function of drama.

It occurs to me that I may have chosen to place this material on the inescapably private in the concluding section of my book because it allows me a shift in perspective that I have felt I needed to make. In writing about drama over the years, I've tended to emphasize, for what have seemed to me good reasons, that the knowledge of theater performance is a "group" knowledge—that is, that it is shaded for individual audience members by the fact that it happens in a group. Not that the group possesses it *as* a group, as a single understanding, but that I experience it as happening to *us*. One has only to think of the difference between watching a comedy in an empty theater and a crowded one to grasp the importance of this distinction.

But I believe one must supplement this awareness of audience knowledge, of the public inflection of theatrical experience, with the resonances that speak more directly, more separatingly, to the *intimus*. Watching Nicholas Hytner's production of *Twelfth Night* at Lincoln Center, I was surprised to find that at the end, where I had always felt that Feste's concluding song accompanies the audience in its transition to everyday reality, Hytner (supported by the shimmering "practicable" waters of Bob Crowley's vast, intensely colored set) instead seemed to return us—me—to the depths of privacy: not to the professional world where Feste, no longer a character, is now the hardworking actor who will "try to please us every day" but to the shifting, liquid recesses of fantasy where our identifications carry on their endless movement of doubling and desire—the depths of fantasy and longing activated by Hytner's very beautiful and certainly very faithful production.

Hytner was in touch with a truth of the play, and it made me see a corresponding truth of theater—that one must not think of its appeal to the communal without also thinking of its arousal of the private. And I think that the heartbreaking beauty of *Twelfth Night* has not a little to do with this. The storms and tempests that beat at the edges of the golden bubble of Illyria, making it float and rise, seeming to create and sustain it even as they threaten, are the wind and rain of our own desires, the great gusts that spring from our being what Handke describes as "alive and alone at the same time."

And so I have wanted to conclude with the private end of the spectrum—to do justice to drama's, as it were, lyric affinity for the "deep of the mind," and not only in order to remind us of tragedy and the limitations of human experience. In the end I am not sure that we want to call them limitations, certainly not as plays like *Ohio Impromptu* treat them. Is it only a trick of this book's rhetoric that by now "inescapable privacy" immediately suggests "inescapable intimacy"? For, as my discussion of privacy and intimacy, especially in their theatrical manifestations, has tried to suggest, the creative reach into the depths of the mind is also a reach outward toward encounter with others, toward the sustaining inwardness of the face-to-face.

We shake hands, as over a vast. One thinks of the great moment in the *Iliad* when the women weep over Patroklos, but each thinks of the private sorrow in her heart, a moment echoed later, at the most important interpersonal moment in the poem, when Priam and Achilles weep together, but Priam weeps for Hektor and Achilles for his father and his friend. And one recalls how important is *boustrophedon* in the *Iliad,* the plowing movement, up the field and back. Self and Other, actor and character, we and they, comedy and tragedy, what is outside the boundary and what within, do not fuse—but they are joined, we are joined, under a presiding face of our own joint creation, in a negotiation, an active co-presence, which encourages us to go on. Each weeps (or laughs) for his own sorrow but over a field of many folk—audience, actor, character, memories—a field of mutually sustained intimacies and identifications, an occasion that offers a permeable boundary, a living verge, into which, like the plowman, we can move and return.

Notes

Page 3. " 'Those earthly . . . what they are.' " *Love's Labor's Lost,* I.i.88–91. All Shakespeare citations are to *The Complete Signet Classic Shakespeare,* gen. ed. Sylvan Barnet (New York, 1972).

Page 4. "Derrida recognizes that. . . ." Jacques Derrida, "La Loi du genre," trans. Avital Ronell as "The Law of Genre," in *Acts of Literature,* ed. Derek Attridge (London, 1992), 223–52.

Page 4. "Alastair Fowler's very useful . . . point." In *Kinds of Literature: An Introduction to the Theory of Genres* (Cambridge, MA, 1982).

Page 5. "We experience [genre] as something . . . like . . . a weather, an attitude, a mood." Benjamin is the critic who comes closest to this book's sense that genre is perceived more as atmosphere or tone than as a set of rules. But, though Benjamin appears to have well understood the experience of genre, his concern when he turns to the subject, especially in *The Origin of German Tragic Drama,* is with genre as a way of categorizing literary procedures after the fact.

Lyotard's view of what he calls "genres of discourse" suggests a possible application to the experience of literary genre, in that it is action oriented. But for Lyotard the action of a discourse finally is subordinate to the rules that produce the action. In the end Lyotard's genres are systems of rhetorical classification, language games for which rules may be supplied. See his discussion in *The Differend: Phrases in Dispute,* trans. Georges Van Den Abbeele (Minneapolis, 1988), esp. 128–50.

Heather Dubrow, in her valuable handbook *Genre* (London, 1982), makes the suggestion that "Genres are strikingly similar to human personalities" (7). There is a way in which this interesting insight could be adapted to the view of drama that is developed in these pages, but this does not appear to be the way that Dubrow's sense of the subject lies. More important, it is not a direction that surfaces anywhere in her study of major trends, past and present, in the understanding of genre—nor is this due to any lack of comprehensiveness or fairness on her part. Many critics are, of course, aware, as Dubrow points out, that narrow and rigid definitions of genre are inadequate. But her book makes clear that, even when these writers acknowledge the looseness or approximateness of genre distinctions, they still approach them as a source for some kind of categorization, a structure for signaling probabilities—a code for what is likely or not likely to happen. This is certainly a reasonable approach to the semiotics of drama. But it leaves crucial features of the experience of genre untouched.

When Dubrow offers as the opinion of "several critics" of this type the idea that "generic codes frequently function like tones of voice rather than a clear cut signal" (106)—again from my point of view a very suggestive formulation—it quickly becomes plain that she, and they, are not really comparing genre to a tone of voice as a lived experience but, rather, to a code of classification or probability that can be *derived* from a tone of voice. It is not a question of murmurs, barks, or insinuations but of "norms" and "models," to use two of her favorite terms.

My ultimate point about genre, however, is not that a sense of norm and model is wholly inappropriate to its study but that this categorizing impulse has been mislocated in relation to dramatic experience. What seems to have been neglected is the degree to which the experience of genre typically *feels like* an experience of boundedness, of category, of exclusion and rule—though, as this study will suggest, that experience is in fact a kind of enabling illusion.

Dubrow's book remains an excellent guide, and again I hope it is clear that I have no quarrel with other students of genre. I simply wish to advance a notion that perhaps lies somewhat outside the traditional boundaries of inquiry.

Page 9. "Aristotle's awareness . . . discoveries about *philia.*" In the *Poetics* Aristotle defines *recognition* as a movement from ignorance to knowledge of family bonds (*Poetics* 1452a30 ff.). See Gerald Else, *Aristotle's Poetics: The Argument* (Cambridge, MA, 1957), 349–50.

Page 9. "Early in the *Poetics.* . . ." *Poetics* 1448b.

Pages 10–11. "'I am Dionysus . . . against my mother.'" Trans. William Arrowsmith, *The Complete Greek Tragedies,* ed. David Grene and Richmond Lattimore, vol. 4 (Chicago, 1960), ll. 1–10.

Page 12. "'*Heko Dios . . . Dionysos.*'" Following Gilbert Murray's text as reprinted (substantially) by E. R. Dodds (Oxford, 1960).

Page 12. "'Good evening . . . excuse me.'" Performance Group, *Dionysus in '69,* ed. Richard Schechner (New York, 1970), n.p.

Page 13. "Euripides introduces a Messenger." *Bacchae,* ll. 677–774.

Page 14. "As Stanley Cavell points out. . . ." *Must We Mean What We Say?* (New York, 1969), 327–30.

Page 15. "'dances . . . living men.'" Arrowsmith, 544. Cf. *Bacchae,* 20–22.

Page 15. "Dionysus . . . will stand revealed . . . in the city." Ibid., 21–22, 47–48.

Page 17. "'CADMUS: First raise . . . in your hands?'" Ibid., ll. 1264–77.

Page 18. "Years ago, I suggested. . . ." *The Actor's Freedom: Toward a Theory of Drama* (New York, 1975), 123.

Page 18. "'The action . . . always carry.'" Ibid.

Page 19. "As Diana Fuss points out. . . ." *Identification Papers* (New York, 1995), 2.

Page 20. Dionysus, Pentheus, and their mothers. Recent classical scholarship is well aware of the complex implications of this kind of feminization in the *Bacchae*. As Froma Zeitlin has observed, Euripides' Dionysus has the power to bring out the suppressed feminine Other in the male personality. (See Zeitlin, "Playing the Other: Theatricality and the Feminine in Greek Drama," *Playing the Other: Gender and Society in Classical Greek Literature* [Chicago, 1996], 341–74.) But by its very neatness our modern Freudian conception of a "female component" or a singular "Other" may elide the more fragmentary and evanescent play of specific identifications in all human identity, male and female. Dionysus and Pentheus, so significantly defined by their god-intoxicated mothers, bring out the fearful theatricality at the base of the self-constructive project. Both characters present us with public thrustings forward of the self that are impossible to separate from inner tearings apart.

Page 20. "Both identity and imitation seem to be born . . . rapidly altering perspectives." See Daniel Stern, *Diary of a Baby* (New York, 1990), 61–63. For fuller clinical documentation, see Stern, *The First Relationship: Infant and Mother* (Cambridge, MA, 1977).

Pages 23–24. "'Consider Admetus . . . unreality of spirits.'" *The Birth of Tragedy,* in The Birth of Tragedy *and* The Case of Wagner, trans. Walter Kaufmann (New York, 1967), 66.

Pages 24–25. "'This process . . . origin of drama.'" Ibid., 64.

Page 26. "As Meredith Skura points out." *The Literary Use of the Psychoanalytic Process* (New Haven, CT, 1981), 265–66.

Page 27. "'Gentle Astringer.'" *All's Well That Ends Well,* V.i.6.

Pages 27–28. "'A gentleman, a stranger' . . . Gentle Ostringer." See *All's Well That Ends Well,* ed. G. K. Hunter (London, 1959), 125.

Page 28. "'*Enter a Messenger* . . . our merriment.'" *Love's Labor's Lost,* V.ii.712–15.

Page 28. "'Worthies, away . . . to cloud.'" Ibid., 720.

Page 28. "'To move . . . impossible.'" Ibid., 853–54.

Page 28. "'Our wooing . . . not Jill.'" Ibid., 872–73.

Page 29. "'That's too long . . . a play.'" Ibid., 876.

Page 29. "'In sooth . . . so sad.'" *The Merchant of Venice,* I.i.1.

Page 29. "'I pray . . . mistress of.'" *As You Like It,* I.ii.1–3.

Page 30. "'A pair of . . . lovers.'" *Romeo and Juliet,* prologue, 6.

Page 30. "'The fearful . . . death-marked love.'" Ibid., 9.

Page 30. "'My mind . . . fearful date.'" Ibid., I.iv.106–8.

Page 31. "'From jigging . . . of war.'" Marlowe, *1 Tamburlaine,* prologue, 1–3, in *The Plays of Christopher Marlowe,* ed. Leo Kirschbaum (New York, 1962).

Page 32. "'sights of power.'" Ibid., V.i.475.

Page 38. "'self-conscious marking . . . of tragedy.'" Simon Goldhill, *Reading Greek Tragedy* (Cambridge, 1986), 244.

Page 39. "Athenian 'tragic moment.'" Jean-Pierre Vernant, in Vernant and Pierre Vidal-Naquet, *Tragedy and Myth in Ancient Greece,* trans. Janet Lloyd (Sussex, England, 1981), 1–5.

Page 39. "'Sick as you are . . . than I.'" *Oedipus the King,* trans. Robert Fagles, in *Sophocles: The Three Theban Plays* (New York, 1982), 142.

Page 40. "'We have to become murderers . . . ourselves as real.'" Gregor von Rezzori, *The Death of My Brother Abel,* trans. Joachim Neugroschel (New York, 1985), 303.

Page 47. "'mirth in funeral . . . dirge in marriage.'" *Hamlet,* I.ii.12.

Page 50. "The actor enters the text." See Michael Goldman, "*Hamlet:* Entering the Text," *Theatre Journal* 44 (1992): 459–60.

Page 51. "'The conclusion which . . . all mere signs.'" Wittgenstein, "The Blue Book," in *The Blue and Brown Books: Preliminary Studies for the "Philosophical Investigations,"* 2d ed. (New York, 1960), 4.

Page 56. "'This is becoming . . . Not enough!'" *Waiting for Godot* (New York, 1954), 44a.

Page 57. "'*He suddenly bends* . . . fire in me now.'" *Krapp's Last Tape and Other Dramatic Pieces* (New York, 1960), 27–28.

Page 58. "'*L [Listener] seated at table . . . Long white hair.*'" *Rockaby and Other Short Pieces* (New York, 1981), 27.

Pages 60–61. "'READER: So the sad . . . *Fade out.*'" Ibid., 34–35.

Page 61. "'a deep of the mind.'" W. B. Yeats, *Essays and Introductions* (New York, 1961), 224–25.

Pages 63–64. "'Flow denotes the holistic . . . present and future.'" Victor Turner, *From Ritual to Theatre: The Human Significance of Play* (New York, 1982), 55–56.

Page 64. "'There is no dualism . . . makes him stumble.'" Ibid., 56.

Pages 66–67. "'Bergner *is combing* . . . *lie behind her.*'" Peter Handke, *The Ride across Lake Constance,* trans. Michael Roloff (New York, 1976), 105.

Page 67. "'To look on . . . at the Globe.'" Shaw, *Our Theatres in the Nineties* (London, 1931), 3:138.

Page 69. "'[The characters] . . . more and more.'" *Ride across Lake Constance,* 158.

Pages 70–71. "'*They all hunch up* . . . *stage becomes dark.*'" Ibid., 158–59.

Page 75. "'The subpoenas issued . . . violations of privacy.'" Jeffrey Rosen, "Annals of Law: Is Nothing Private?" *New Yorker,* June 1, 1998, 36–37.

Pages 75–76. "as Jeffrey Rosen has pointed out." Ibid., 38.

Page 77. "'Thus conscience . . . of us all.'" *Hamlet,* III.i.83.

Page 80. "Gregers and Hedvig or Astrov and Yelena." In *The Wild Duck* and *Uncle Vanya,* respectively.

Page 81. "'How awful it is . . . able to enter.'" Pirandello, *Henry IV,* trans. Mark Musa, in *Six Characters in Search of an Author and Other Plays* (London, 1995), 122.

Page 81. "'The generations stare . . . freeze to death.'" Brecht, *In the Jungle of Cities and Other Plays,* trans. Anselm Hollo (New York, 1966), 83.

Pages 81–82. "'When I stood . . . blotting me out.'" Pinter, *No Man's Land* (New York, 1975), 46.

Pages 83–84. "'PRISONER: Mother, I'm . . . fuck it up.'" Pinter, *Mountain Language* (New York, 1988), 45–47.

Page 85. "'I once knew a madman . . . so unusual.'" *Endgame* (New York, 1958), 44.

Page 86. "'HAMM: Can there . . . no doubt.'" Ibid., 2.

Page 91. Elin Diamond. *Unmaking Mimesis* (New York, 1997).

Page 91. "the . . . view of identification that Brecht puts forward." Ibid., 108–9.

Pages 98–99. The infant's reaction to an expressionless face. See Daniel Stern, *Diary of a Baby* (New York, 1990), 60–61. Infants as young as two-and-a-half months respond to the still-face procedure. See also Stern, *The Interpersonal World of the Infant* (New York, 1985), 149.

Page 99. "As Shakespeare's Duncan . . . warns us." "There's no art / To find the mind's construction in the face." *Macbeth*, I.iv.11–12.

Page 100. "'Preexisting the plane of ontology is the ethical plane.'" Lévinas, *Totality and Infinity: An Essay on Exteriority*, trans. Alphonso Lingis (Pittsburgh, 1969), 201.

Page 101. "As one commentator puts it. . . ." Sean Hand, *The Lévinas Reader* (Oxford, 1989), 88.

Page 102. "'Language . . . could not commence.'" Lévinas, *Totality and Infinity*, 202.

Page 102. "'The [full face] conjuncture . . . irreducible to totality.'" Ibid., 80.

Page 103. "'moon of comic tradition.'" Yeats, *The Collected Plays* (New York, 1953), 423.

Page 105. "Ben Jonson–like." On more than one occasion Jonson attacked *The Winter's Tale* for its improprieties. This was part of his general quarrel with Shakespeare, but it's clear that *The Winter's Tale* really got under his skin.

Page 106. "'ANTIGONUS: Blossom . . . *by a bear.*'" *Winter's Tale,* III.iii.45–57.

Page 107. "Sidney's very example. . . ." *Sidney's Apologie for Poetrie,* ed. J. Churton Collins (Oxford, 1907), 52.

Pages 108–9. "'What you do . . . are queens.'" *Winter's Tale,* IV.iv.135–46.

Page 109. "'Flora . . . April's front.'" Ibid., 1–2.

Page 110. "Bernard Beckerman's . . . performance and presentation." Beckerman, *Theatrical Presentation* (New York, 1990), 1.

Page 111. "'Oh, she's warm!'" *Winter's Tale,* V.iii.109.

Page 112. "'That she is living . . . she lives.'" Ibid., 115–17; italics mine.

Page 113. "communicating with a dead lover." The text, though not absolutely specific, certainly suggests this relation. Beckett scholarship has proposed a host of startling sources and unlikely allusions, including, amazingly, one to Beckett's sometime employer, James Joyce. In this connection it is worth noting a 1981 conversation that James Knowlson had with Beckett about the play:

> We spoke first of the link with Joyce . . . I then told him that I had heard the "dear face" who is evoked by the Reader referred to as if it too were the face of Joyce. "It is a woman, isn't it?" I asked. "It's Suzanne [Beckett's wife]," he replied. "I've imagined her dead so many times. I've even imagined myself trudging out to her grave." (James Knowlson, *Damned to Fame: The Life of Samuel Beckett* [London, 1996], 665)

Page 114. "'With thee, beloved . . . of one dying.'" Nietzsche, unused MS note for the posthumously published "Philosophy in the Tragic Age of the Greeks," quoted in James Miller, *The Passion of Michel Foucault* (New York, 1993), 11. Beckett could have read the original in Nietzsche's *Werke,* ed. Naumann (Leipzig, 1894 ff.), 10:147, which Miller cites. I have moved the first sentence of the paragraph to the end of the quotation, separated by ellipses, to allow the reader to follow the sequence of my discussion more easily. Actually, the sequence as it occurs in Nietzsche provides additional evidence for influence since the idea of a dying self isolated in its own narration echoes one of Beckett's recurrent themes and would thus have been even more likely to catch his eye.

Page 116. "'deep of the mind.'" See above, page 126.

Page 117. "'[shake hands] as over a vast.'" *Winter's Tale,* I.i.32.

Page 118. "'try to please us every day.'" *Twelfth Night,* V.i.409.

Page 119. "'alive and alone at the same time.'" *The Ride across Lake Constance,* 103.

Index